The Palgrave Concise Historical Atlas of Central Asia

D1556466

To my wife, Alfia Abazova

The Palgrave Concise Historical Atlas of Central Asia

Rafis Abazov

THE PALGRAVE CONCISE HISTORICAL ATLAS OF CENTRAL ASIA
Copyright © Rafis Abazov, 2008.

First published in 2008 by
PALGRAVE MACMILLAN™
175 Fifth Avenue, New York, N.Y. 10010 and
Houndmills, Basingstoke, Hampshire, England RG21 6XS
Companies and representatives throughout the world.

PALGRAVE MACMILLAN is the global academic imprint of the Palgrave Macmillan division of St. Martin's Press, LLC and of Palgrave Macmillan Ltd. Macmillan® is a registered trademark in the United States, United Kingdom and other countries. Palgrave is a registered trademark in the European Union and other countries.

ISBN-13: 978–1–4039–7541–6 cloth
ISBN-10: 1–4039–7541–8 cloth
ISBN-13: 978–1–4039–7542–3 paperback
ISBN-10: 1–4039–7542–6 paperback

Library of Congress Cataloging-in-Publication Data

Abazov, Rafis.
    The Palgrave concise historical atlas of central Asia / Rafis Abazov.
        p. cm.
    Includes bibliographical references and index.
    ISBN 1–4039–7542–6
        1. Asia, Central—Historical geography—Maps. 2. Asia, Central—History—Maps. 3. Asia, Central—Antiquities—Maps. I. Title.

G2202.21.S1A2 2008
911'.58—dc22   2007048032

A catalogue record for this book is available from the British Library.

Design by Newgen Imaging Systems (P) Ltd., Chennai, India.

First edition: February 2008

10 9 8 7 6 5 4 3 2 1

Printed in the United States of America.

Contents

Preface

The Central Asian republics have been commanding attention in news rooms around the world since gaining independence in 1991. Importantly, foreign-policy makers and many international relations experts in Moscow, Beijing, Delhi, Istanbul and recently, Washington, D.C., have been claiming that this region, its resources, and its transportation infrastructure are of vital and strategic importance for the globe. The great paradox is that the major world powers, divided by thousands of miles and located in completely different geopolitical environments, have such high stakes in this remote part of the world. The situation is especially puzzling as the United Nations Development Program (UNDP) in its regional report on Central Asia in 2005 put many parts of the region on a par with the poorest countries in the world.

To explain this paradox, we have to open the history textbooks. In the past the region played an important role in the political, military and economic development of Eastern Europe, the Middle East, South and East Asia. For example, one of the most defining military campaigns in world history, which changed the fates of so many countries on the Eurasian continent and led to the establishment of the world's largest empire—the Mongol Empire—was launched from Central Asia. In the nineteenth century the two greatest superpowers of that era—Britain and Russia—vied with each other to establish control over this area of the Eurasian land mass in a competition dubbed the Great Game. The stakes were very high, and poor knowledge of the Central Asian geopolitical terrain and its history cost the players dearly: The Russian Empire lost nearly half of its expeditionary army in its campaign in Khiva in 1840, while the entire British expedition corps was slaughtered on the outskirts of Kabul in 1842. In the early twenty-first century U.S. military strategists misinterpreted terrorist threats from the Al-Qaida base in Afghanistan, and that miscalculation led to the largest terrorist act on U.S. soil in the history of the United States, thus forcing the American government to revise its policy toward Central Asia by establishing the first U.S. military bases in the region. In addition, in the present day, the Central Asian republics control the second largest oil, gas and uranium ore resources on the territory of the former Soviet Union.

Historical and geographical maps can help us understand many of these paradoxes, events and geopolitical considerations. For example, most of the Central Asian capitals are situated just three or four hours' flight time from Beijing, Moscow, Delhi or Tehran. Because of their strategic location and numerous historical, cultural, political and economic relations, and their relatively large diasporas spread across neighboring countries, developments in Central Asia also greatly affect the Russian central provinces, the Xingjiang province of China, Afghanistan, Iran and even such distant regions as Iraq and Turkey.

Many questions are currently arising: What role did Central Asia play in world history and what role does it play now? How have Central Asian states interacted with world powers in the past? What can we learn from the geopolitical and historical development in the region? How does the geographic location affect the economic development of the region? This set of easy-to-read historical maps was developed with such questions in mind, in order to depict the geopolitical and geoeconomic dynamics of different eras and the rich and intricate history of the Central Asian region.

The primary purpose of this atlas is to provide students and the general public with an effective tool that will help them visualize historical changes in the Central Asian region. It is also intended to supplement various research and textbooks in Central Asian, Middle Eastern, Eurasian and Russian history. In order to keep the book accessible to a wide audience, however, most of the maps have been developed in a basic format. For specialized maps, tables, and information on economic and political development, climatic changes, transportation infrastructure and other topics, I refer readers to specialized publications—a concise list of which can be found in the selected bibliography section at the end of this book. The atlas is designed to cover a general historical framework, major periods and events in the history of the region, and territorial changes over time; again, for in-depth analysis and research, readers should turn to the specialized literature.

I have followed the same format as other works in the *Palgrave Concise Historical Atlas* series. The maps in this atlas are produced in two colors and only major geographical features are included, such as major terrains, rivers, mountains and cities. Two factors affected this decision— the cost effectiveness and accessibility of the information to the general public.

One-page texts accompany each map, covering certain historical periods and major developments in the relevant geographical area. These specific texts have been written to help readers develop an understanding of the major features of the various historical periods and to stimulate interest in looking for detailed studies in research publications. Due to space limitations, the texts cover only major events and changes and do not go into detailed discussions.

The preparation of this atlas posed three major challenges: differences in interpretation of the historical development in the region; inconsistency in the spelling of various geographic locations; and frequent changes of the names of various geographic locations. The first challenge arises from the fact that interpretations of Central Asian history has often been ideologically and politically motivated both in the West and in the East. The other challenges arise from the fact that the Central Asian alphabets were changed several times during the twentieth century. Until the 1920s, most Central Asians wrote in the Arabic script and used the Persian and Turkic languages in literature, media, local administration and education.

The Soviet government initiated a switch from the Arabic script to the Latin alphabet in the 1920s. In the late 1930s, however, all Central Asian languages switched again, abandoning the Latin for the Cyrillic alphabet. The literary languages were codified and mass education in national languages was introduced. Between the 1940s and mid-1980s the central Soviet government heavily promoted the Russian language as the *lingua franca* in all the Central Asian republics, and most of the geographic and historical maps were produced in Russian. In the late 1980s and early 1990s the Central Asian governments demanded greater use of their native languages. All republics in the region passed new language laws that made their local languages the only state languages in their respective countries and initiated a gradual switch from the Russian to the local language in all areas of life, including state administration and education. Some countries, such as Turkmenistan and Uzbekistan, went even further by abandoning the Cyrillic alphabet and reembracing the Latin.

In addition, the region's urbanization and nation-state building happened largely in the twentieth century and largely during the Russian imperial and Soviet dominations. Therefore, the names of many places, including cities, towns, provinces, and even mountains and canals have been changed frequently due to the political considerations of those eras. Since 1991 a new trend has emerged as the Central Asian governments tried to de-Russify their geographic landscape and to change place names back to the pre-Russian, pre-Soviet eras' designations or to the native spelling. I have tried to address this problem in a separate table on pages xv–xvii.

I would like to acknowledge support from the Harriman Institute at Columbia University, as well as my colleagues and Vladimir Bessarabov of the Cartographic Section, Department of Field Support, United Nations, who generously shared their knowledge and expertise. I would also like to thank Anthony Wahl, Senior Editor, Alan Bradshaw, Production Director, and Kate Ankofski, Editorial Assistant, at Palgrave Macmillan. However, any errors are the author's sole responsibility.

RAFIS ABAZOV
Harriman Institute,
Columbia University,
New York

General Key to the Maps

All of the maps were initially prepared in black and white and reflect only those features that are most important for the specific historical periods. The shaded areas and colored lines were added in order to highlight important historical and geopolitical changes. Due to the nature of the work, none of the maps are intended to endorse any geopolitical or border claims and were designed only to illustrate the most important historical developments. The maps use the following key unless otherwise indicated:

International boundaries	———
Provincial boundaries	—·—·—·
Names of states	**KYRGYZSTAN**
Names of regions	**MAVERANAHR**
Names of ethnic groups	Kazakhs
Names of rivers	*Syr Darya*
Names of lakes	*Lake Balqash*
Names of national capitals	❂ Dushanbe
Names of cities	Mary
Conflict areas	☙

Acronyms and Abbreviations

ADB	Asian Development Bank
BPSR	Bukhara People's Soviet Republic
CIA	Central Intelligence Agency
CIS	Commonwealth of Independent States
CP	Communist Party
CPC	Caspian Pipeline Consortium
CPSU	Communist Party of the Soviet Union
ECO	Economic Cooperation Organization
EEC	Eurasian Economic Community
EIU	Economist Intelligence Unit
FDI	foreign direct investments
FTZ	free trade zone
GDP	gross domestic product
HDI	Human Development Index
IMF	International Monetary Fund
IMU	Islamic Movement of Uzbekistan
Kazakh SSR	Kazakh Soviet Socialist Republic
KGB	Komitet Gosudarstvennoi Bezopastnosti (Committee on State Security)
Kolkhoz	*kollektivnoye khozyaistvo* (collective farm)
KPSR	Khorezm People's Soviet Republic
Kyrgyz SSR	Kyrgyz Soviet Socialist Republic
NATO	North Atlantic Treaty Organization
NGO	non-governmental organization
OIC	Organization of the Islamic Conference
OSCE	Organization for Security and Cooperation in Europe
PRC	People's Republic of China
RSFSR	Russian Soviet Federated Socialist Republic
SCO	Shanghai Cooperation Organization
Sovkhoz	*sovetskoye khozyaistvo* (Soviet farm)
Tajik SSR	Tajik Soviet Socialist Republic
TASSR	Turkistan Autonomous Soviet Socialist Republic
TCP	Turkistan Communist Party
Turkmen SSR	Turkmen Soviet Socialist Republic
UN	United Nations
UNDP	United Nations Development Program
UNESCO	United Nations Educational, Scientific, and Cultural Organization
USSR	Union of Soviet Socialist Republics
Uzbek SSR	Uzbek Soviet Socialist Republic
WTO	World Trade Organization

Changes in Geographical Names

During the twentieth century, a significant number of geographic names were modified several times, including the names of countries, capitals, provinces and major cities due to various political changes. This process accelerated in the 1990s, as the Central Asian republics gained their independence. One of the most important issues in the preparation of this work was that of consistency, as many of Central Asia's geographic names can be found in various spellings. The names of many cities and provinces can be found in different spellings on different historical maps: The name of the capital of Turkmenistan can be found in four different forms—Askhabad, Ashkhabad, Ash'habat and Ashgabat; the name of the province center in Kyrgyzstan can be found in four different forms—Dzhalal-Abad, Zhalal-Abad, Jalal-Abad and Jalalabad; the name of a province in Uzbekistan can also be found in four different forms—Fergana, Ferghana, Farhona and Farghona. There are many factors that affected these transformations. Several major changes in the usage of the script in the Central Asian republics generated issues of transliteration of various words and terms within the Central Asian languages and from Central Asian to foreign languages as well. The Central Asian languages were largely standardized only in the twentieth century, with considerable influences of Russian and European linguists and scholars. Finally, since the 1990s the Central Asian republics have been undergoing a process of de-Russification of geographic terms, personal names and academic and technical terminology. This process has not yet been completed, and therefore different spellings are found in different reference sources and on different maps.

This reference table provides examples of major changes in the geographic names of countries, capital cities and provinces. All new geographic names are written according to the contemporary local spelling.*

* In order to keep consistency, the author used a single reference source: https://www.cia.gov/library/publications/the-world-factbook/

Kazakhstan

Before 1991	After 1991
Kazakh SSR	The Republic of Kazakhstan (Kazakhstan)
Alma-Ata (capital)	Almaty
Tselinograd	Astana (new capital)
Alma-Ata Province (*oblast*)	Almaty Province
Aktubinsk	Aqtöbe Province
Atyrau	Atyrau Province
Mangyshlak Province	Mangghystau Province
Pavlodar Province	Pavlodar Province
Uzhno-Kazakhstan Province	Ongtüstik Qazaqstan Province
Karaganda Province	Qaraghandy Province
Kustanai	Qostanay Province
Kyzyl-Orda Province	Qyzylorda Province
Severo-Kazakhstan Province	Soltustik Qazaqstan Province
Tselinograd Province	Aqmola Province
Vostochano-Kazakhstan Province	Shyghys Qazaqstan Province
Zhambul Province	Zhambyl Province
Zapadno-Kazakhstanskaya Province	Batys Qazaqstan Province

Kyrgyzstan

Before 1991	After 1991
Kirgiz SSR	The Kyrgyz Republic (Kyrgyzstan)
Frunze (capital)	Bishkek (capital)
Batken District (*raion*)	Batken Province
Chui Province (*oblast*)	Chui Province
Dzhalal-Abad Province	Jalal Abad Province
Issyk-Kul Province**	Ysyk Kol Province
Naryn Province	Naryn Province
Talas Province	Talas Province

Tajikistan

Before 1991	After 1991
Tajik SSR	The Republic of Tajikistan (Tajikistan, also Tojikiston)
Dushanbe (capital)	Dushanbe (capital)
Kurgan Teppe	Khatlon Province
Leninabad Province	Sughd Province
Gorno-Badakhshan Autonomous Province	Kuhistoni Badakhshon Province

** Corrected by author to reflect pronunciation in English.

Turkmenistan

Before 1991	After 1991
Turkmen SSR	The Republic of Turkmenistan (Turkmenistan)
Ashkhabad (capital)	Ashgabat (capital)
Ashkhabad Province (*oblast*)	Ahal Province (*welayat*)
Charjou Province	Lebap Province
Krasnovodsk Province	Balkan Province
Mary Province	Mary Province
Tashauz Province	Dashoguz Province

Uzbekistan

Before 1991	After 1991
Uzbek SSR	The Republic of Uzbekistan (Uzbekistan, Also Ozbekiston)
Tashkent (capital)	Tashkent (capital) (also Toshkent)
Andizhan Province (*oblast*)	Andijon Province (*viloyat*)
Bukhara Province	Bukhoro Province**
Ferghana Province	Farghona Province**
Dzhizak Province	Jizzax Province
Namangan Province	Namangan Province
Navoi Province	Navoiy Province
Kashkadar'ya Province	Qashqadaryo Province
Karakalpak ASSR	Qoraqalpog'iston Republic
Samarkand Province	Samarqand Province
Surkhandar'ya Province	Surkhondaryo Province**
Tashkent Province	Toshkent Province
Khorezm Province	Xorazm Province

I
Introductory Maps

Map 1: Physical Characteristics

The five Central Asian republics—Kazakhstan, Kyrgyzstan, Tajikistan, Turkmenistan and Uzbekistan—form the Central Asian region. This region represents a distinctive geopolitical and geoeconomic entity with its own shared cultural and historical legacy, political and economic boundaries, and demographic dynamics. The region, geographically an uneven pentagon shape, is about the size of half of the continental United States (without Alaska). The coastline of the Caspian Sea forms most of the region's natural western boundary. The mountain ranges of Kopetdag and Pamirs form the southern border of the region, separating Central Asia from Afghanistan and Iran. The mountain ranges of Tian Shan and Alatau form the eastern borders of the region. Vast prairies and forest-steppe form the northern border of the region with Russia. This landlocked region has a land area of approximately 1,542,200 square miles (around 3,994,000 square kilometers).

A region of extremes and contrasts, Central Asia can be subdivided into five major geographical and climatic zones that do not necessarily coincide with national boundaries: the northern steppe and forest-steppe zone; the western dry desert zone; the southern and southeastern high mountain zone; the fertile valleys and oases between the Amu Darya and Syr Darya rivers; and the series of moderately elevated valleys on the border between the high mountains and central plain.

The large flat steppe and forest-steppe of the northern zone cover nearly half of Central Asia and correspond with the territory of Kazakhstan. This zone is a part of the Eurasian steppe that stretches from the Dnepr River in Eastern Europe to the Altai Mountains, and it is characterized by a continental climate with extremely cold winters and warm summers. The temperatures might range from −38°C (−36.4°F) to −14°(7°F) in January, though occasionally it falls to −48°C (−54.4°F), and from +5°C (41°F) to +28°C (82°F) in July.

The dry and water-scarce desert zone of the southwestern areas of Central Asia extends into Turkmenistan and western Uzbekistan. There is little precipitation in both summer and winter, and the extremes of the continental climate—very cold and windy winters and unbearably hot summers with temperatures up to +40°C and +50°C (104°F and 122°F)—render the desert quite inhospitable.

The major highland mountain ranges of the third zone stretch from southeastern Kazakhstan and Kyrgyzstan to Tajikistan and southern Uzbekistan. The highest peaks are situated above 5,000 meters (16,400 feet) and form an uninhabitable chain of mountains often covered with ice, glaciers and permafrost. The climate is more severe at high altitudes (3,000 meters [9,840 feet] and higher), ranging from −40°C (−40°F) to −14°C (7°F) in January and from +5°C (41°F) to +18°C (65°F) in July.

In the fourth zone, the fertile and densely populated valleys and oases between the Amu Darya and Syr Darya rivers encompass Uzbekistan, northern Tajikistan and southwestern Kyrgyzstan. The climate here is relatively mild and dry, with temperatures ranging from −14°C (7°F) to +7°C (45°F) in January and between +22°C (71.6°F) and +29°C (84°F) in July.

In the fifth zone, the series of moderately elevated valleys that begin in Kyrgyzstan, Tajikistan, and Uzbekistan, and continue into southern Turkmenistan make this the most livable area in the region. The weather is also affected by the continental climate, but it is relatively mild and dry, comparable to the climate in the midwestern United States. The temperatures range from −14°C (7°F) to +7°C (45°F) in January and between +26°C (78°F) and +29°C (84°F) in July.

The cultural landscape and population distributions in Central Asia have varied during different historical eras due to several reasons, including climatic change and human activities. In this regard, an imaginary line across the Aral Sea from east to west can divide Central Asia into two parts. To the north of this line is the huge, never-ending Eurasian steppe where people have been mainly engaged in animal husbandry. This steppe has an extremely fragile and volatile ecosystem that is suitable for raising the sheep, horses and camels of nomads and pastoral nomads. To the south of this line, people have been mainly involved in intensive agriculture, growing grains, cotton, fruits and vegetables, rendering animal husbandry of secondary importance. Many scholars argue that large portions of what are now the Karakum and Kyzylkum deserts also were prosperous cultivated lands that became desert due to a combination of climatic changes and environmental mismanagement.

The geopolitical importance of Central Asia arises from the fact that it is a meeting point for three major world religions and civilizations—Buddhism, Islam and Christianity. Military historians cite plenty of examples when major campaigns against the Indian subcontinent, China and Russia were undertaken through the territory of Central Asia. The strategic importance of Central Asia was elegantly highlighted in the early twentieth century by Sir Halford John Mackinder, the British political geographer, who produced a simple geopolitical formula: "Who rules the Heartland [which included Central Asia] commands the World-Island [Eurasian continent]. Who rules the World-Island commands the World."

For nearly two thousand years, Central Asia was an important crossroads for international trade along the Silk Road that connected East Asia with the Middle East and Europe. The region was also important for lucrative trade between the Indian subcontinent and Eastern Europe, including the Bulgar and Kazan khanates, Kievan Rus and Muscovite Russia.

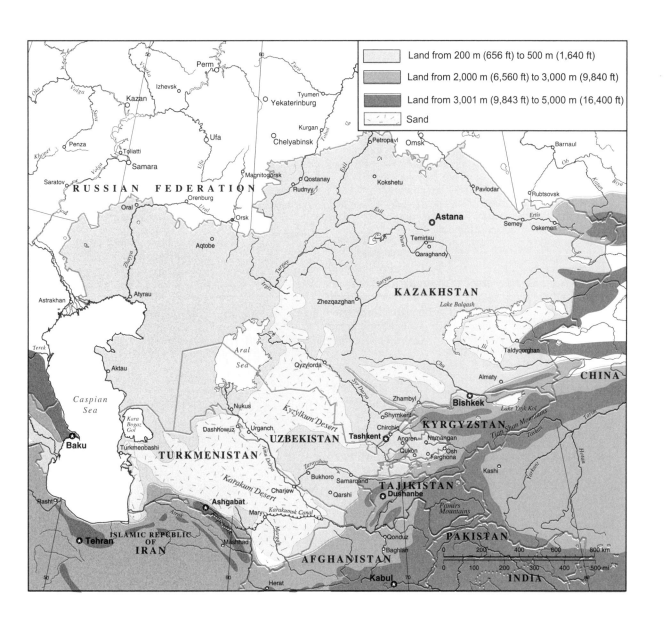

Map 2: Political Characteristics

The modern external borders of the Central Asian region were established in the late nineteenth century as the result of a formal arrangement between the British and Russian empires. This arrangement ended the bitter competition for political and military control in the region. The British expanded their influence over the territory of Afghanistan and Iran, and the Russian Empire established its influence over the land to the north of these two states, in the process extending its control to the Kokand and Khiva khanates and the Bukhara emirate.

The present administrative shape of Central Asia was established in the mid-1920s during the region's national delimitation. The Kremlin introduced administrative delimitation in the Central Asian region and embraced the ideas of those Central Asian leaders who suggested dividing the region along vague ethnic lines. On 27 October 1924 the Central Executive Committee (a branch of the Soviet government) issued a decree on the delimitation of the Central Asian region and establishment of the Soviet Socialist Republics.

Kazakhstan
Capital: Astana
Area in sq. mi. (sq. km): 1,049,175 (2,717,400)
Population: 15,285,000—July 2007, CIA est.
Ethnicity (%): Kazakh (64.4), Russian (20), Ukrainian (3.7), Uzbek (2.5), German (2.4), Tatar (1.7), Uigur (1.4), other (3.9)—2007 est.
Languages: Kazakh, Russian, Uzbek
Religions (%): Muslim (70), Russian Orthodox (24), Protestant (2), other (4)
Type of Government: Emerging presidential democracy
Gross Domestic Product (GDP): $53.6 billion—2006, CIA est.
GDP by Sector (%): agriculture (6.8), industry (39.5), services (53.7)—2007, CIA est.
Main Exports: oil and oil products, ferrous metals, gas, chemicals, machinery, grain, wool, meat, coal

Kyrgyzstan
Capital: Bishkek
Area in sq. mi. (sq. km): 76,640 (198,500)
Population: 5,284,149—July 2007, CIA est.
Ethnicity (%): Kyrgyz (68), Uzbek (13.8), Russian (9.5), Dungan (1.1), Ukrainian (1.0), Uygur (1.0), other (5.7)—2007 est.
Languages: Kyrgyz (official), Russian (official), Uzbek, Kazakh
Religions (%): Muslim (84), Christian (11), other (5)
Type of Government: Emerging presidential democracy
Gross Domestic Product (GDP): $2.255 billion—2006, CIA est.
GDP by Sector (%): agriculture (34.5), industry (19.5), services (46)—2006, CIA est.

Main Exports: cotton, wool, meat, tobacco, gold, mercury, uranium, hydropower, machinery, leather

Tajikistan
Capital: Dushanbe
Area in sq. mi. (sq. km): 55,252 (143,100)
Population: 7,076,598—July 2007, CIA est.
Ethnicity (%): Tajik (79.9), Uzbek (15.3), Russian (1.1), Kyrgyz (1.1), other (2.6)—2000 census
Languages: Tajik, Uzbek, Russian
Religions (%): Sunni Muslim (90), Shi'a Muslim (5), other (5)
Type of Government: Emerging presidential democracy
Gross Domestic Product (GDP): $2.066 billion—2006, CIA est.
GDP by Sector (%): agriculture (23.4), industry (28.6), services (48.0)—2005 est.
Main Exports: aluminum, electricity, cotton, fruits, vegetable oil, textiles

Turkmenistan
Capital: Ashgabat
Area in sq. mi. (sq. km): 188,445 (488,100)
Population: 5,097,028—July 2007, CIA est.
Ethnicity (%): Turkmen (85), Uzbek (5), Russian (4), other (6)
Languages: Turkmen, Uzbek, Russian
Religions (%): Muslim (92), Christian (6), other (2)
Type of Government: Emerging presidential democracy
Gross Domestic Product (GDP): $15.18 billion—2006, CIA est.
GDP by Sector (%): agriculture (17.7), industry (39.2), services (43.2)—2006, CIA est.
Main Exports: gas, crude oil, petrochemicals, cotton fiber, textiles

Uzbekistan
Capital: Tashkent
Area in sq. mi. (sq. km): 172,745 (447,400)
Population: 27,780,059—July 2007, CIA est.
Ethnicity (%): Uzbek (80), Russian (5.5), Tajik (5.0), Kazakh (3.0), Karakalpak (2.5), Tatar (1.5), other (2.5)—2007 est.
Languages: Uzbek, Tajik, Russian, Karakalpak
Religions (%): Muslim (88, mostly Sunni), Christian (9), other (3)
Type of Government: Emerging presidential democracy
Gross Domestic Product (GDP): $10.83 billion—2006, CIA est.
GDP by Sector (%): agriculture (31.1), industry (25.7), services (43.2)—2006, CIA est.
Main Exports: cotton, gold, energy products, mineral fertilizers, ferrous metals, textiles, food products, automobiles

Map 3: Natural Resources

Many areas in Central Asia have difficult terrains, tough climates and fragile environments. Together these factors expose the population to natural disasters, climate fluctuations and other upheavals beyond human control. Mother Nature seems to have compensated by endowing Central Asia with various natural resources.

The most indispensable resource has been an abundance of both arable land and pastures. The fertile soil in numerous oases has helped to sustain the commercial-scale growth of various crops, including silk, cotton, fruits, vegetables and berries. Vast pasturelands have provided an excellent ground for raising horses, which were vital for warfare before the industrial revolution and a highly prized export object. Some chronicles report that at the peak of trade, between 50,000 and 100,000 horses a year were exported from the Eurasian steppe to China, India and Persia.

Central Asia is also endowed with mineral resources, including gold, silver, copper, iron ore and various jade stones that have been mined and processed since the first millennium B.C. The local craftsmen acquired considerable skills and achieved technological advancements, though the industrial revolution and major technological changes arrived in the region only in the nineteenth and twentieth centuries. In the early and mid-twentieth century local companies discovered huge reserves of oil and gas. All those resources, however, are distributed unevenly throughout the region.

Kazakhstan possesses the richest and most diverse mineral resources among the Central Asian republics. The region's largest oil and gas deposits lie in the western and southern provinces of the country. Kazakhstan's potential oil reserves range between 100 and 150 billion barrels. In 2005 Kazakhstan was in thirteenth place in the world in proven oil reserves, ahead of the United Kingdom, the United States and Mexico. Gas reserves range between 1.8 and 2.5 trillion cubic meters. Kazakhstan also has large commercial deposits of coal, iron ore, chrome ore, cobalt, copper, molybdenum, gold, uranium and other metals that are situated largely in the eastern and northeastern provinces of the country. Kazakhstani farmers cultivate various cereals on the vast prairies of the country and herd sheep, horses, camels, goats and cows. In the southern provinces the farmers cultivate such valuable export crops as cotton, tobacco, various fruits and vegetables.

Kyrgyzstan is a mountainous country that consists of three distinct parts: northern, southern and highlands. In the valleys in northern Kyrgyzstan the farmers cultivate cereals, vegetables and tobacco. In the valleys of southern Kyrgyzstan the climate is excellent for growing cotton, tobacco, various fruits and berries. In the highlands the herders raise sheep, horses, goats and yaks.

The country has very small deposits of oil and gas that range between 10 and 50 million barrels of oil and 5.6 and 10 billon cubic meters of gas. Kyrgyzstan also possesses significant deposits of antimony, gold, mercury, coal, uranium and other minerals. The country's hydroelectric power resources are considerable, as large reserves of fresh water can be found in the glaciers and mountain lakes. In fact, Kyrgyzstan is in third place in the CIS (after Russia and Tajikistan) for potential hydroelectric power resources.

Tajikistan's mountains cover nearly 90 percent of the land, making many areas in the country unsuitable for commercial agriculture. In the valleys in the northern and southern provinces the farmers cultivate highly valued export quality cotton, fruits, tobacco, vegetables and berries. Tajikistan is the second largest producer of silk among CIS members after Uzbekistan. The country has very small deposits of oil and gas that range between 12 and 50 million barrels of oil and 5.6 and 10 billon cubic meters of gas (2006, official est.). In addition, Tajikistan has significant deposits of antimony, gold, mercury, coal, silver, uranium and other minerals. The total silver deposits range between 40,000 and 60,000 tons.

Turkmenistan's vast plains are largely unsuitable for commercial agriculture due to lack of water. Yet, the herders raise camels, high quality horses, and sheep that are famous for their wool and fur (karakul). In the southern, southeastern and eastern provinces of the country, farmers are engaged in intensive agriculture, raising cotton, cereals, fruits and vegetables. Turkmenistan possesses huge reserves of oil and gas. Its oil reserves are the fourth largest among CIS members and range between 1.0 and 2.0 billion barrels (2005, CIA est.), with potential oil reserves reaching between 10 and 25 billion barrels. Its proven gas reserves range between 3.0 and 5.0 trillion cubic meters, with potential gas reserves reaching between 20 and 30 trillion cubic meters. In fact, the country was the world's ninth-largest gas exporter in 2005 (2005, CIA est.).

Uzbekistan's agriculture benefits from its warm climate, abundance of sunshine and the availability of irrigation water in major valleys across the country. The country is among the world's largest producers of cotton and silk. The farmers also cultivate fruits, vegetables, cereals and berries for domestic consumption and for exports to the regional markets. The herders raise livestock including sheep, cows, bulls, goats and camels. Uzbekistan's proven oil reserves are between 0.6 and 2.0 billion barrels, with potential oil reserves ranging between 2.0 and 3.0 billion barrels; its gas reserves range between 2.2 and 3.5 trillion cubic meters. Uzbekistan also has large commercial deposits of gold, coal, copper, molybdenum, silver, uranium and other metals.

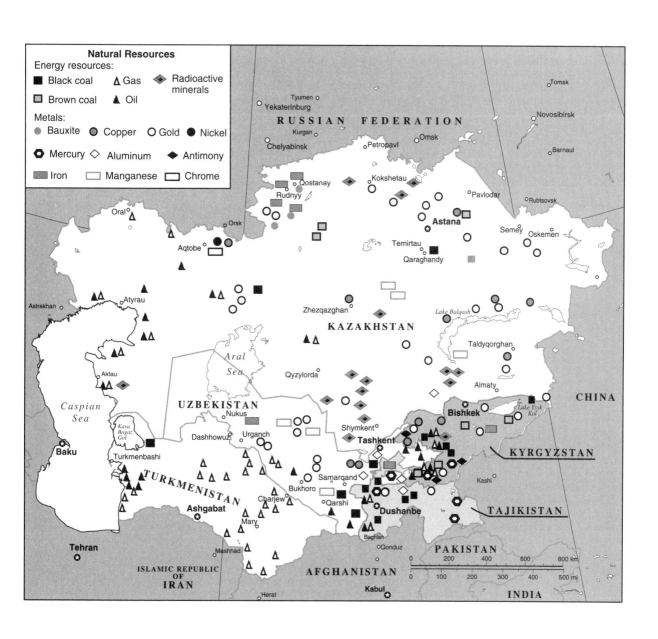

Map 4: Demography

In the past, the population size, structure and composition of Central Asia were probably very different from what they are today. For centuries Central Asia was a region where people of Turkic-Mongol, Indo-Arian and Middle Eastern origin mixed in a giant melting pot. Probably, the size of the population peaked between the fourth and second centuries B.C., the fifth and seventh centuries A.D., the eleventh and thirteenth centuries and the fourteenth and fifteenth centuries. This fluctuation can be seen in the fate of the city of Samarqand (now in Uzbekistan). According to various chronicles, Samarqand's population reached about 20,000 in the second century B.C., 50,000 in the fifth to sixth century A.D., 100,000 to 200,000 in the eleventh century, declined to about 50,000 in first half of thirteenth century, climbed to about 300,000 in the early fifteenth century, and dwindled to just 1,000 families in the early eighteenth century; the city grew to 50,000 in the nineteenth century. In 2007 its population reached 412,000 according to an official estimate.

The Central Asian republics, like many countries in the Third World, experienced rapid population growth in the twentieth century. The population of Central Asia was estimated to be 57 million in 2007, up from between 7 and 10 million in 1905. Today it is comparable in size to that of France, Britain or Turkey. It is expected that this population figure will double by 2050. If that happens, it would be roughly the projected population of Japan (100 million) or Russia (105 million).

The *Kazakhs* belong to an ethnic group of about 11 million people. They make up the majority of the population of Kazakhstan (about 63 percent) according to an official estimate in 2007. Kazakhs also reside in China, Mongolia, Russia, Kyrgyzstan and Uzbekistan. Most of the Kazakhs are Sunni Muslims. The Kazakhs in rural areas have preserved a strong tribal identity, which is much weaker among the urban populations.

The *Kyrgyzs* (also Kirgizs, Kara-Kyrgyzs) make up the majority of the population of Kyrgyzstan (about 68 percent); they also live in Afghanistan, China, Kazakhstan, Tajikistan and Uzbekistan. Their total number in the region is between 4.5 and 5.0 million people. Until 1926 they were also known as the *Kara-Kyrgyzs*. Most of the Kyrgyzs are Sunni Muslims. The Kyrgyz tribal identity is deeply embedded in the psychology of the people.

The *Tajiks* (also *Tojiki*) belong to an ethnic group of about 7 million people who live mainly in Tajikistan and have large diasporas in Afghanistan, Uzbekistan, Kazakhstan and Russia. The Tajiks are the only non-Turkic speaking people in Central Asia, as their language, Tajiki, is close to Iranian. Many Tajik families are bilingual and speak various Turkic languages. The overwhelming majority of the Tajiks are Sunni Muslims, though there is an influential community of Ismailis, linked to the Shi'a teaching of Islam.

The *Turkmens* (also Turkomans) belong to an ethnic group of about 5 million people that make up the majority of the population of Turkmenistan; they also live in Afghanistan, Iraq and Iran. Traditionally, Turkmen society is divided into several tribes and tribal groups. Most of the Turkmens are Sunni Muslims. The tribal identity is still essential for the Turkmens and it plays a significant role in national politics. The Turkmens speak the Turkmen language, one of the languages of the Oguz linguistic group of the Turkic language family.

The *Uzbeks* are the largest ethnic group in the region, comprising approximately 25 million people. Most Uzbeks (over 20 million) live within the territory of Uzbekistan, though large Uzbek communities—each exceeding a million—live in neighboring Central Asian countries and in Afghanistan. The overwhelming majority of the Uzbeks are Sunni Muslims. Historically, the territory of what is now Uzbekistan was one of the most urbanized areas in the region, the "land of a thousand cities." The Uzbek nation was formed by two quite different groups of people: the settled, Persian-speaking population of Bukhara, Samarqand and other cities and towns, and the Turkic-speaking pastoral-nomadic population.

The *Karakalpaks* (or Qaraqalpaqs) are an ethnic group of about 650,000 people according to a 2006 official estimate. They mainly live in the Karakalpakistan Republic (an autonomous entity within Uzbekistan), which occupies the northwestern part of Uzbekistan. The overwhelming majority are Sunni Muslims.

The *Russians* constitute the largest ethnic minority group in the Central Asian region, though their numbers have been steadily declining since 1991. According to various estimates, there will be between 4.5 and 6 million Russians total in 2008 in the five Central Asian republics, down from about 9.5 million in 1989. In 2007 there were about 4 million in Kazakhstan, 700,000 in Uzbekistan, 330,000 in Kyrgyzstan, 120,000 in Turkmenistan and 50,000 in Tajikistan. An overwhelming majority of the Russians are Orthodox Christians. Central Asian Russians live mainly in the major metropolitan areas where they arrived in large waves of immigration in the nineteenth and twentieth centuries.

There are many other large and small ethnic groups in Central Asia. Some of the groups, such as the Iranians, Turks, Arabs, Kurds, Tatars, Uigurs, and others arrived in the region many centuries ago, settling in large and small towns and cities and becoming inseparable parts of the Central Asian nations. Others, such as the Germans, Ukrainians, Koreans and Poles, moved in mainly during the twentieth century; they still maintain their distinctive cultures and speak their own languages at home.

Map 5: Central Asian Cultures

The cultures of the Central Asian people have been formed through centuries of interactions among several traditions. The region has been a meeting point for different civilizations—Zoroastrian, Buddhist, Islamic and Christian. It has also been an area of active contact between nomads and sedentary people, and it has been an intersection of Turkic and Persian cultures. In the past, with the exception of the loose Mongol Empire, there was never a single political entity that controlled the entire region in its present boundaries. Various parts of the Central Asian region were affiliated with different states, empires or civilizations.

For many centuries religious discourse and interchange were of great importance for the spiritual development of Central Asian societies. These factors shaped multifaceted cultures and traditions. Many religious thinkers of the ancient and medieval worlds found in Central Asia both a refuge and an inspirational environment for developing and refining their thinking. Central Asians played an important part in the development of Zoroastrian, Buddhist, Manichean, Eastern Christian and Islamic theological and legal thought, philosophy and culture. Such philosophers and theologians as Al-Bukhari, Al-Farabi, Al-Khoresmi, Al-Beruni, Al-Ghazali, Nakhshbandi and Akhmed Yasavi have been widely recognized in the Muslim world.

The millennium-long division of the Central Asian population into nomads and settlers has had a major role in defining political and cultural identities. Notably, the nomads shared and preserved many ancient Turkic and Mongol traditions. Throughout the centuries some of these Turkic mores made a significant impact on some aspects of cultural development in the Persian-speaking world. The Islamic and Persian cultural traditions in turn immensely influenced the Turkic-speaking communities in the region. Indeed, the Turkic and Persian elements are intermingled to such a degree that some scholars are inclined to use the term "Turkic-Persian" instead of "Central Asian" in reference to the region's cultural heritage.

The Central Asian region has been traditionally subdivided into three cultural cores.

The first historical core of Central Asia is situated in the river basins of and the oases between the two greatest waterways of the region. One river is the Amu Darya (*Oxus* in Latin and *Jayhun* in Arabic sources), which begins in the Pamirs Mountains in the far southeast corner of Central Asia and takes its precious water to the west for 500–600 miles (804–965 kilometers), before turning to the north and ending in the Aral Sea. The area on the right bank of the river was traditionally called Maveranahr ("the area beyond the river" in Arabic). The other river is Syr Darya (*Iaxartes* in Greek and *Sayhun* in Arabic sources), which begins in the Tian Shan Mountains and flows to the northwest for about 500 miles (750 kilometers), then turns to the west and heads to the Aral Sea. Eventually the name Maveranahr began to be used to refer to the area between these two rivers.

The second historical core of Central Asian pastoral civilization was situated to the northeast of the Syr Darya River. It was called in Turkic *Jetysuu* ("the area of seven rivers"). During the early medieval era many cities flourished in this area flanked by the Tian Shan Mountains in the south and Lake Balqash in the north, including Otrar, Balasagun and Taraz. This area was completely devastated during the Mongol invasion.

The third area that played a significant role in Central Asian history is the Eurasian steppe. This land roughly corresponds with the vast territory from the Russian Altai Mountains in the east all the way to the Volga River in the west. For many centuries numerous pastoral and pastoral-nomadic tribes raised horses, sheep, goats and camels here, utilizing the steppe's practically endless supply of grass.

Three other areas that played no less a role in ancient Central Asian history have been cut off from the region in the modern era by political events. One is *Khorasan* ("the land of rising sun" in Persian). In the past it was a large area to the south and southwest of the Amu Darya River in the eastern part of the Iranian plateau and included the cities of Herat, Nishapur and Merv. Khorasan was one of the centers of cultural and political development of the sedentary people in Central Asia and of the interaction between Persian and indigenous Central Asian cultures. The second area is the area of the Tarim River basin (also sometimes called Eastern Turkestan). It is situated to the east of the Tian Shan Mountains and its oases are watered by the Tarim, Kashgar and many other rivers. The Eastern Turkistan area played a prominent role in the political and cultural development of Central Asia, especially during the first millennium A.D., as a center of Buddhist and Manichean civilizations. The third area is the steppe zone that stretches from the Jetysuu area to southern Siberia and Mongolia. This was the realm of many Turkic and Mongol tribal leaders for centuries and was often used as a base for military campaigns in Central Asia and in the Eurasian steppe.

Then, in the nineteenth and twentieth centuries, an entirely different cultural universe—Russian, Soviet and Western—swooped through the region. Central Asian societies, which have unique historical, cosmological and metaphysical roots in preindustrial society, came under the influence of the value systems of the industrial and postindustrial world.

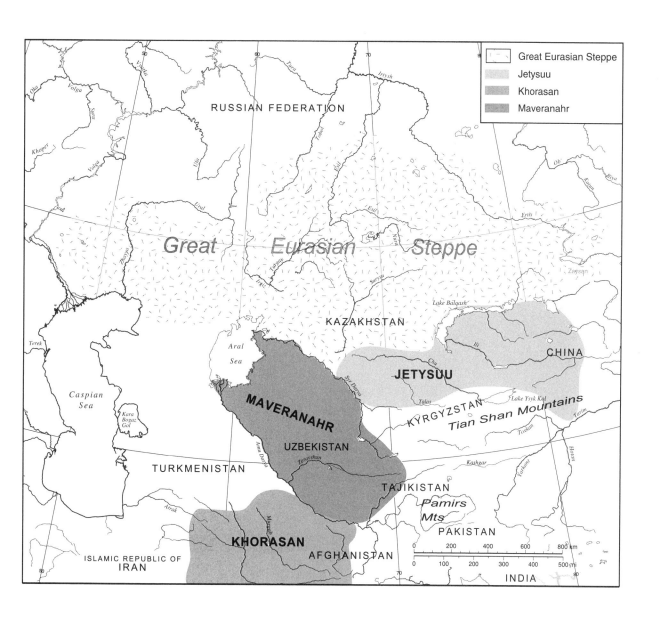

II

Early History, Sixth Century B.C. to Sixth Century A.D.

Map 6: Political Map of the Ancient World

With the rise of the ancient civilizations that organized people into complex societies with distinct cultures, social and political institutions, religious traditions and governing systems, humans began interacting with each other in more systematic ways. Trade, technological and cultural exchanges, wars and international alliances affected communities far away from the major centers of the ancient era. It may be said that world history was born during this epoch.

The place of Central Asia in ancient world history is very difficult to define (Adshead 1993). However, existing evidence suggests that during the eleventh to seventh centuries B.C. the population of Central Asia was already engaged in various forms of crop cultivation and animal husbandry. Moreover, there was a division of labor into two large groups. One was represented by settlers who cultivated fertile soil in numerous oases on and around the Zeravshan, Murgab and Amu Darya (Oxus in ancient Greek chronicles) rivers and their tributaries. As early as this period, Central Asians introduced irrigation techniques that helped to establish and maintain relative prosperity in their lands. The other group was represented by the nomadic and seminomadic population of the vast steppe to the north of the Syr Darya River. During these centuries these peoples domesticated and actively traded their animals (horses, camels, sheep, goats and bulls) with settled populations in exchange for grain, weapons, metal work and manufactured goods.

Between the eighth and sixth centuries B.C. the early ancient states and protostates had emerged in the Transoxiana (the area between the Amu Darya and Syr Darya rivers), the earliest appearing at the Farghona, Murgab, Bukhara, Khwarezm and other oases. From the sixth to the third centuries B.C. Central Asian peoples had established several principle urban centers on sites close to present-day Samarqand (in Uzbekistan), Balkh (in Afghanistan), Merv (in Turkmenistan), Khojand (in Tajikistan) and many other cities. Some of the cities were quite large, at times supporting populations in the tens of thousands. Other cities and towns were relatively small, as their citizens were exclusively engaged in subsistence and small-scale commercial agriculture and barter trade.

These urban centers were in one way or another linked to the major world powers of the ancient era, as gold and jade originating from Central Asia were found in China and Persia. In the ancient era the Central Asians dealt with four great neighboring powers—Persia, China, Mediterranean states and Scythia—who would eventually play important roles in the history of Central Asia.

The early Persian states were situated in the neighborhood immediately to the south of the major Central Asian cities. From early times they were linked to some of the original Central Asian city-states through intensive trade and cultural exchange. The Persian rulers regularly launched relatively minor and at times considerably larger wars and campaigns to the north in order to expand their direct and indirect control over this area. For example, in 530 B.C. the Persian King Cyrus II the Great (ca. 590–530 B.C.) campaigned in Central Asia but was defeated by an army led by Queen Tomiris. However, Darius II returned a decade later with a larger army and conquered Central Asia, turning Bactria, Parthia, Khwarezm, Ariana and Sogdiana into Persian satrapies and recruiting Central Asian cavalry into the Royal Persian army.

The Mediterranean or western powers were situated far to the west. About 2,000 miles (3,300 kilometers) separated the major Central Asian cities from the early Greek city-states in the Mediterranean. Yet the Greeks expanded their numerous trade outposts and colonies in all directions, and evidence suggest that they reached as far east as present-day Iran, Afghanistan and Uzbekistan. Herodotus (ca.484–425 B.C., the "father of history"), indicates that the Greeks knew about the development of the Persian and Scythian worlds (modern Central Asia) and their traders, spies, missionaries, scholars and adventurers regularly reached some parts of Central Asia (Herodotus 1963).

Major ancient Chinese cultural and political centers were between 2,000 and 2,400 miles (3,300 and 3,900 kilometers) east of Central Asia. They were separated not only by great distances, but also by wild and impenetrable deserts, steppe and mountains populated by powerful nomadic and seminomadic tribes. Many adventurers, traders and scholars traveled to and fro nonetheless, and by the sixth century B.C. the Chinese already had a relatively clear cultural and political portrait of the Central Asian lands. The ancient Chinese historian Sima Qian (ca.145–85 B.C.) was able to describe land to the west of China with considerable accuracy using earlier chronicles and reports.

The powerful though unstable Scythian tribal confederations of the vast Eurasian steppe formed an independent political force that played an important role in the history of the Central Asian city-states. Scythian political and military activities were especially visible when capable and ambitious leaders emerged, bringing formidable forces under their control. At the same time they contributed immensely to the economic development of Central Asia as they supplied valuable goods for the region and for international trade. Ancient historical chronicles suggest that the Scythians were engaged with the Persians and Greeks both militarily and commercially.

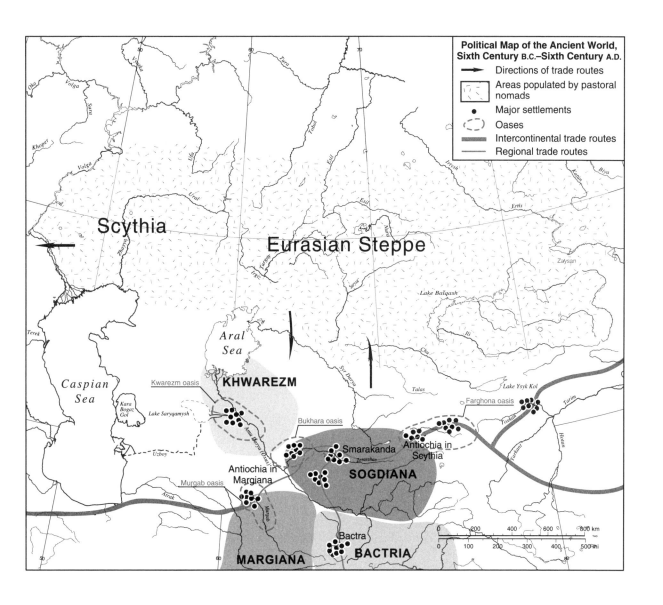

Political Map of the Ancient World, Sixth Century B.C.–Sixth Century A.D.

- Directions of trade routes
- Areas populated by pastoral nomads
- Major settlements
- Oases
- Intercontinental trade routes
- Regional trade routes

Scythia

Eurasian Steppe

Aral Sea

Caspian Sea

KHWAREZM

Kwarezm oasis

Bukhara oasis

Smarakanda

Antiochia in Scythia

Farghona oasis

SOGDIANA

Antiochia in Margiana

Murgab oasis

MARGIANA

Bactra

BACTRIA

Map 7: Bactria, Sogdiana, Margiana and Khwarezm, Sixth to Third Centuries B.C.

During the sixth century B.C., the early ancient states began consolidating in the territory of Central Asia. Geoclimatic and geopolitical factors played important roles in this process. The ancient states solidified around the urban centers that were established and developed in the fertile oases and on the banks of the major rivers: Amu Darya (Oxus in ancient Greek chronicles), the upper basin of Syr Darya (Iaxartes), Zeravshan (Polytimetus), Murgab (Marg) and others. In the dry continental climate those rivers provided access to clean irrigation and drinking water. At the same time, the mountains, hills and deserts provided important defensive positions against sudden attacks from the nomads.

The political and cultural life of the region during this era was concentrated mainly in the southern areas. In this regard, the Amu Darya River, which rises in the Pamirs mountains, played a similar role in the rise of Central Asia's civilizations as did the Nile River in North Africa or the Euphrates and Tigris in Mesopotamia.

Bactria (also Bakhtar in Persian, Bhalika in Arabic and Ta-Hsia in Chinese) emerged on the upper streams of the Amu Darya and the Balkh River. Its capital, Bactra, was probably situated in a valley where the city of Balkh (also Vazirabad) now lies in the Balkh province in northern Afghanistan. The high mountains around the Bactrian center provided excellent defense against surprise attacks from troublesome neighbors and good staging posts for territorial expansions. At its peak, Bactria controlled significant areas of what are now southern Tajikistan and Uzbekistan, and northern Afghanistan. The ancient state was consolidated during the sixth to fourth centuries B.C., though the Persian Empire under the Achaemenid dynasty brought Bactria under its control. Its prosperity was built on intensive agriculture in the oases and banks of the rivers, the mining of jade and metals in the mountains, and profitable barter trade with its neighbors. Some scholars believe that Zoroastrianism was founded there in the sixth century B.C., as its founder, Zarathushtra, lived in Bactria.

Sogdiana (Sughuda in Persian and Sute in Chinese) emerged in the territory that corresponds with the middle reaches of the Amu Darya and Zeravshan rivers. Sogdiana was situated to the north of Bactria and was probably a loose alliance of city-states with centers in ancient Samarqand (Smarakanda), Bukhara, Khojand and others. At its zenith, Sogdiana expanded its control to include the area that is now southern Uzbekistan, Tajikistan, western Kyrgyzstan and northern Afghanistan, though it is not clear if these territories were ever united into a single political entity during that period. The prosperity of the Sogdian cities was built on intensive agriculture, animal husbandry, mining and the skills of its craftsmen and merchants. They also profited from the export of jade and jade jewelry and the re-export of silk in later eras. Between the sixth and fourth centuries B.C. the Sogdian city-states struggled against the Persian Achaemenian empire but were eventually defeated.

Margiana emerged at the oases of the lower reaches of the Murgab River. Situated to the west of Bactria and Sogdiana, it was a strategically important entrepôt for regional and transcontinental caravans traveling from Persia to Central Asia and further to China. The prosperity of Margiana was built on extensive agriculture and the financial and trading services provided by the numerous caravans. Although Margiana lost its political independence to the Persian Empire probably in the mid-sixth century B.C., it continued to enjoy a significant level of political and economic autonomy. Alexander the Great founded a city in Margiana named after himself—Alexandria in Margiana (later Antiochia in Margiana)—which became one of the largest and most prosperous cities in the area.

Khwarezm (Khwarazm in Persian and Hualazimo in Chinese) emerged about the lower waters of the Amu Darya River. Khwarezm, likely one of the oldest political entities in the territories of Central Asia, was situated between Sogdiana and the Aral Sea. It was probably a loose confederation of settled and seminomadic groups. In the mid-sixth century B.C. the Persian King Cyrus II (ca. 590–530 B.C.) brought the area into his empire as a protectorate, although the extent of Persian control is not very clear. The prosperity of Khwarezm was built on intensive agriculture, animal husbandry and regional trade with the nomads.

The Eurasian steppe was not united into a single political entity, and during this period early nomadic protostates began emerging in this territory. The area was populated by Sarmatian and Scythian tribes (these names are at times used interchangeably), who controlled land from southern Siberia to the Black Sea. These nomadic and seminomadic tribes built their prosperity on animal husbandry and active exchanges, both through trade and military campaigns alongside their neighbors. Some scholars believe that on many occasions ancient Scythians were militarily allied with the Persian and Greek empires. In fact, it was Sarmatian female warriors who inspired the Greek tales of the Amazons. Recent archeological discoveries indicate that these Scythians built quite sophisticated and prosperous societies, and the many gold artifacts found in their burial grounds indicate that they had developed a unique culture and art while being aware of Persian, Chinese and Mediterranean artistic achievements.

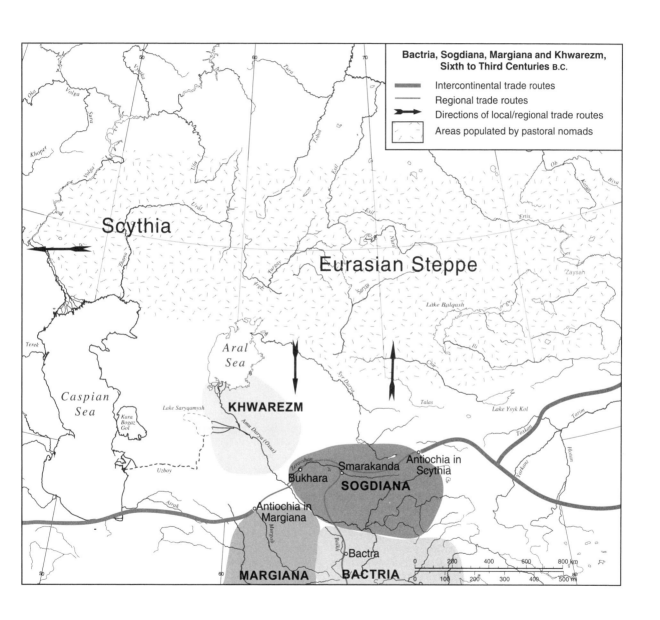

Bactria, Sogdiana, Margiana and Khwarezm, Sixth to Third Centuries B.C.

	Intercontinental trade routes
	Regional trade routes
	Directions of local/regional trade routes
	Areas populated by pastoral nomads

Scythia

Eurasian Steppe

Caspian Sea

Aral Sea

Lake Saryqamysh

KHWAREZM

Lake Balqash

Kara Bogaz Gol

Uzboy

Lake Ysyk Kol

Amu Darya (Oxus)

Bukhara

Smarakanda

Antiochia in Scythia

SOGDIANA

Antiochia in Margiana

Arak

Bactra

MARGIANA

BACTRIA

Terek

Khoper

Volga

Oka

Sura

Volga'

Vitta

Tura

Tobol

Esil

Irtis

Ob

Ketun

Biya

Zaysan

Ertis

Ili

Chu

Talas

Syr Darya

Naru

Sarysu

Esil

Tobol

Ujil

Uril

Turgay

Irgiz

Leravshan

Margab

Bukhi

Tarim

Tarkani

Toxkan

Hotan

| 0 | 200 | 400 | 600 | 800 km |
| 0 | 100 | 200 | 300 | 400 | 500 m |

Map 8: Alexander the Great and the Greek Influence in Central Asia

Events in the mid-fourth century B.C. seriously disrupted the political development of Central Asia and changed the course of history for several centuries. In the eyes of Central Asians, the Greek-Macedonian army led by Alexander the Great (356–323 B.C.) probably came out of nowhere. He appeared from the west to move triumphantly through Mesopotamia and Persia, defeating the Persian army, one of the world's most powerful military forces until that time. Alexander successfully fought against the Persian garrisons, campaigning between 330 and 327 B.C., and then suddenly left the region and never returned.

The political situation in Central Asia, along with its economic development, on the eve of Alexander's invasion contributed significantly to his success. The Persian Achaemenian empire had controlled the Central Asian states in one way or another for about 200 years. By the mid-fourth century this control was already significantly weakened. The centralized Persian Empire had been considerably undermined by internal strife, excessive expenditures on the royal family's lavish court life, public constructions and numerous military campaigns that siphoned revenues from a shrinking state budget. On top of that, there was growing strife between the center and the Central Asian periphery over taxes and the recruitment of conscripts and mercenaries into the Persian army.

Alexander the Great probably entered Central Asia in 330 B.C., after campaigning in Persia for about four years in pursuit of the Persian King Darius III (380–330 B.C.). Darius III gathered large armies several times but lost all the decisive battles. Step by step he retreated further to the east, probably hoping that the remoteness of his Central Asian satrapies would give him shelter against the advancing Greek troops. However, entrepreneurial Greek merchants, craftsmen and colonists had probably settled in or visited Central Asia and were able to provide help to Alexander. Darius's military mismanagement and mediocrity angered many of his followers and supporters. In 330 B.C. he was murdered by his own governor Bessus, the satrap of Bactria. Bessus declared himself Darius's successor and adopted the name Artaxerxes V.

With the rise of Bessus-Artaxerxes V as a self-nominated ruler of the Persian Empire, the war entered a new stage. Alexander and his army faced the threat of a protracted guerrilla war in the difficult mountainous terrain of Bactria and later Sogdiana, where Bessus-Artaxerxes V sought refuge. Bessus's lack of legitimacy undermined his standing with the army and he too was murdered, in 329 B.C., by his own followers. The war did not quite end there, for Spitemenes, a satrap of

Sogdiana, rose to lead the local resistance. He in turn was killed by his own followers in 328 B.C.

Alexander decided that his positions were strong enough and he turned to conquer India. Before leaving for India, however, he decided to cement his stand in the region by making some strategic arrangements, one of which was a dynastic marriage. In 327 B.C., by accident or by an accord, he met and married Princess Roxana (Roshanak—"little star" in Persian), the daughter of an influential local leader and one of the most beautiful women in Asia. Other arrangements included the establishment of several cities as Greek-Macedonian strongholds and colonies. Ancient sources traditionally report that Alexander established six such centers in Central Asia: Alexandria of Margiana (near present-day Merv in Turkmenistan); Alexandria of Ariana (near present-day Herat in northern Afghanistan); Alexandria of Bactria (near present-day Balkh in northern Afghanistan); Alexandria on the Oxus (on the upper reaches of Amu Darya, which the Greeks called Oxus); Alexandria of Caucasum (close to present-day Bagram in northern Afghanistan); and Alexandria Eschatae (near present-day Khojand in northern Tajikistan).

Bactria and Sogdiana were included in Alexander's world empire, though very soon after his death in 323 B.C. these provinces began experiencing political turmoil. The empire was shattered by internal instability and infighting and rivalries among his generals. Between 301 and 300 B.C. Seleucus, one of Alexander's generals, consolidated his control over the Persian possessions and founded the Seleucid Empire. In 250 B.C. Diodotus, governor of Bactria, broke away from the Seleucids and established an independent Greco-Bactrian kingdom. This kingdom flourished for 125 years, between 250 and 125 B.C., as an island of Hellenism in Central Asia. The Greco-Bactrian state prospered and became known as the land of a thousand cities, leaving significant cultural marks among both the settled and nomadic populations of Central Asia. At its zenith it extended its control well into Sogdian territory in the north and to areas of northern India, although it struggled against militant nomadic tribes that regularly attacked the kingdom from the north.

The final blow to the Greco-Bactrian kingdom came from the Eurasian steppe, where powerful nomadic tribal confederations of the Huns and Yueh-Chih fought fiercely for influence in the second century B.C. The Yueh-Chih lost to the Huns and were forced to move to the territory between the Syr Darya and Amu Darya rivers, eventually regaining strength and destroying the Greco-Bactrian state, probably between 126 and 120 B.C.

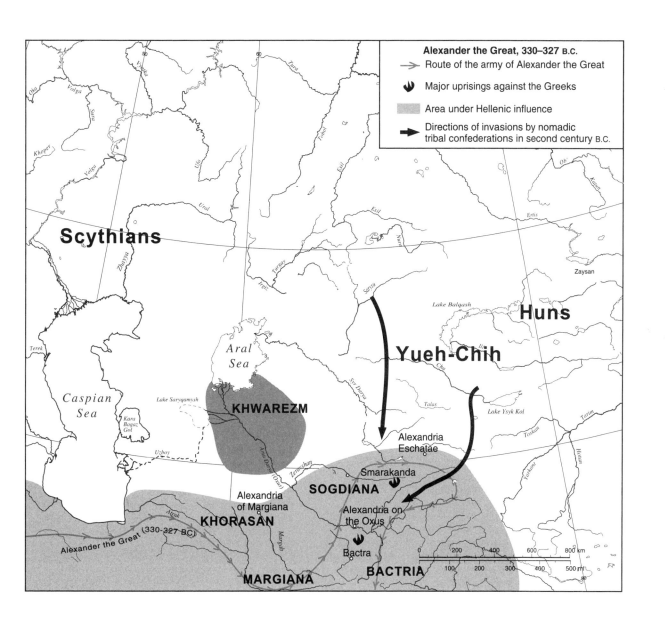

Alexander the Great, 330–327 B.C.

→ Route of the army of Alexander the Great

Major uprisings against the Greeks

Area under Hellenic influence

➡ Directions of invasions by nomadic tribal confederations in second century B.C.

Scythians

Khoper

Volga

Sura

Volga

Ufa

Ural

Terek

Caspian Sea

Kara Bogaz Gol

Aral Sea

Lake Saryqamysh

Uzboy

KHWAREZM

Amu Darya (Oxus)

Zerovshan

Alexander the Great (330-327 BC)

Atrak

KHORASAN

Alexandria of Margiana

Murgab

MARGIANA

Bactra

Alexandria on the Oxus

BACTRIA

SOGDIANA

Smarakanda

Alexandria Eschatae

Syr-Darya

Talas

Lake Ysyk Kol

Toskan

Yorkant

Hotan

Tarim

Yueh-Chih

Huns

Lake Balqash

Ili

Chu

Zaysan

Ob'

Ertis

Esil

Saryu

Nura

Turgay

Irgiz

Tobol

Tura

Esil

Zhevya

0   200   400   600   800 km

100   200   300   400   500 mi

Map 9: Parthian Empire and the Kushans

The Parthian state emerged around 250 B.C. and lasted for nearly 500 years, becoming one of the longest empires in ancient history. At its height, the kingdom of Parthia controlled territory from the Caspian Sea and southern Caucasus in the north, Bactria in the east, the Persian Gulf in the south and Mesopotamia in the west. Its rulers actively exchanged diplomatic and trade missions with the Chinese, Roman Empire and Central Asian states, and during the age of the Parthian Empire the ancient Great Silk Road reached its peak. The Parthians entered the annals of western history for some of the most remarkable military battles in history: They defeated the renowned legions of the Roman general Crassus in 53 B.C. and inflicted heavy losses upon Mark Antony (83–30 B.C.) in 36 B.C., ultimately leading to his downfall and death along with his lover, the legendary Cleopatra.

The early Parthian State was founded by a small confederation of Iranian-speaking tribes, who probably lived to the north and around the Kopetdag Mountains in what is now southern Turkmenistan. In about 250 B.C. a tribal king, Arsuces, established a small semi-independent principality. Step by step he spread his control over cities and towns to the south. However, it was not until Mithridates the Great (ruled ca. 171–138 B.C.) and Phraates II (ca. 138–127 B.C.) that the Parthian state truly became a world empire. The Parthians benefited from the demise of the Greco-Bactrian state and the Seleucid Empire in the second century B.C. The Parthians moved the center of political gravity further to the west, defeating Seleucid armies and gradually reaching the Persian Gulf and Mesopotamia. Their ambitious military campaigns and territorial expansions alarmed the Roman Empire. In 53 B.C. the Roman general Crassus invaded Parthia from the west but lost his entire army at the Battle of Carrhae. Allegedly, most of the captured Roman soldiers were sent to settle in various places in Central Asia. Roman forces managed to defeat the Parthians and even to kill their king in 39 B.C., but Mark Antony experienced heavy losses during a campaign three years later. Frequent wars between the Parthians and Rome ultimately contributed to the decline of both empires.

Neither the Parthian Empire's longevity nor all its military successes would have been possible without its excellent administrative organization of the state. The empire's decentralized nature was one of its major strong points (Colledge 1967), and this derived from the tribal background of the dynasty, its adaptation to Hellenic traditions, and the incorporation of peoples from various ethnic backgrounds, including Assyrians, Greeks, Persians, Jews and Sarmatians, into one political entity. The ruler of the empire was often called the King of Kings (in Persian *Shah-n-Shah*)—he was considered first among equals, with numerous members of the royal family scattered around the Empire and enjoying significant autonomy. On the economic front, the Parthian rulers always patronized international and regional trade providing transportation infrastructure, military security and stable taxes and tariffs. Even in times of military conflict and wars, the Parthian rulers did not interfere with the caravan trade, letting goods flow without restrictions between the East and the West.

Skill in the diplomatic arts also contributed to the rise and strengthening of the empire. Its rulers maintained stable and friendly relations with China and regularly exchanged diplomatic missions, sometimes of several hundred people, with the Chinese emperor. The Parthians were also actively engaged with the Scythians of the Eurasian steppe to the north of the Aral Sea. It is likely that the two parties competed on some issues, especially over control of their bordering territories, but both benefited from the regional trade and exchanges.

The rise of the Kushan kingdom, which emerged from the remnants of the Greco-Bactrian state in the first half of the first century A.D., complicated the geopolitical situation in Central Asia. The Kushans probably belonged to one of the Yueh-Chih tribal confederations, and their political power was based on their control of areas of present-day Afghanistan. The Kushan dynasty was founded between 1 and 30 A.D. and strengthened under King Kajula Kadphises (30–80 A.D.). The state reached its height under King Kanishka I (ruled 127–147 A.D.), and extended its control from the Amu Darya River basin in the north to the Indus River basin in the south. Unfortunately the historical chroniclers did not leave us a detailed account of interactions between the Parthians and Kushans, the two natural rivals for influence in Central Asia. It is probable that the Kushans fought the Parthians over influence in Transoxiana.

By the third century A.D. it was becoming clear that Parthia was exhausted by its never-ending wars with the Romans, and that its human and financial resources were overstretched. Various Parthian provinces gradually began demanding more autonomy while contributing fewer taxes and fewer military units to the imperial cause. The final blow came between 198 and 224 A.D., when a combination of military misfortune in the latest war with the Romans and revolts by the vassals in various parts of the empire, including Central Asia, led to the ultimate fall of the Parthian dynasty.

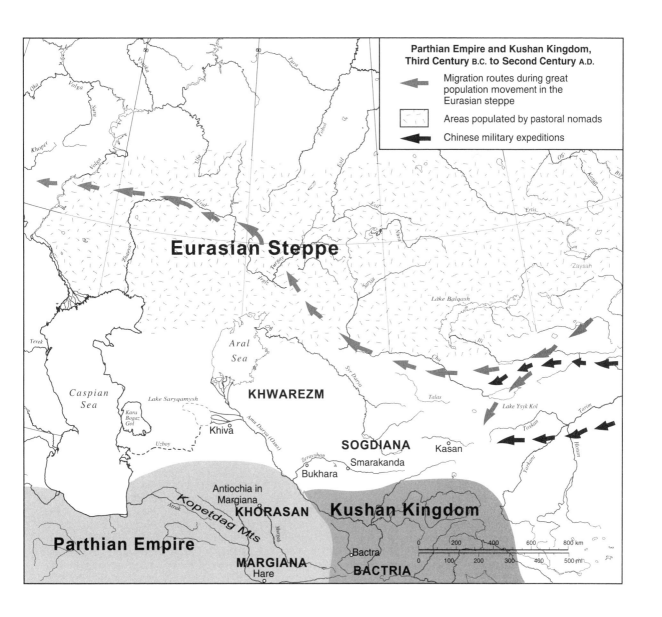

Parthian Empire and Kushan Kingdom, Third Century B.C. to Second Century A.D.

→ Migration routes during great population movement in the Eurasian steppe

▢ Areas populated by pastoral nomads

→ Chinese military expeditions

Eurasian Steppe

Caspian Sea

Aral Sea

KHWAREZM

Lake Balqash

Lake Ysyk Kol

SOGDIANA

Kasan

Smarakanda

Bukhara

Khiva

Antiochia in Margiana

KHORASAN

Kushan Kingdom

Parthian Empire

Kopetdag Mts

MARGIANA

Hare

Bactra

BACTRIA

Terek

Caspian Sea

Kara Bogaz Gol

Lake Saryqamysh

Uzboy

Amu Darya (Oxus)

Zerayshan

Syr Darya

Talas

Chu

Ili

Tarim

Toskan

Yarkant

Hotan

Zaysah

0   200   400   600   800 km
0   100   200   300   400   500 mi

Map 10: Sassanid Empire, Third to Seventh Centuries

The political situation surrounding Central Asia changed considerably during the third century A.D., affecting both political and economic relations with the region's neighbors. In the south the fall of the Parthian Empire and, shortly after, that of the Kushan Empire was followed by several decades of intense wars. In the East, the Chinese Empire of the Han Dynasty (206 B.C.–220 A.D.) disintegrated and was replaced by several kingdoms that were engaged in unceasing military strife. The Chinese not only withdrew from Central Asia and Turfan (present-day China), but also reduced trade with all their trading partners. In the north, on the great grasslands of the Eurasian steppe, the new tribal confederations of the Turkic-speaking peoples gained strength in and around Greater Mongolia and southern Siberia. They began slowly moving westward, pushing various groups of Iranian-speaking tribes to move to the Transoxiana, Caucasus and Eastern Europe.

In 224–226 Ardashir I (?–241), ruler of one of the Parthian provinces, defeated the last emperor of the Parthian Empire. He established a new Sassanid dynasty and accepted the title of *Shah-n-Shah* (King of Kings). This dynasty would rule for the next 425 years, until 651. Ardashir I and his son Shapur I (ruled 241–272) paid considerable attention to Central Asia and areas surrounding it. They campaigned in Khorasan, Margiana, Khwarezm, Bactria and probably in Sogdiana against the last Kushans (see maps 8 and 9).

The region prospered under the Sassanids, expanding its irrigated fields and profiting from regional trade with its nomadic neighbors. Due to the instability of China, however, the transcontinental trade along the Great Silk Road shrank significantly. Yet there were important changes afoot that would contribute immensely to the economic well-being of Central Asia for many centuries. In about the second century (although some sources indicate it was the third century), silk cocoons were secretly brought from China to Central Asia, probably to the Farghona Valley. Entrepreneurial Central Asian farmers mastered production of the cocoons, and craftsmen learned to produce silk materials. It is not clear how long it took to perfect the new technologies, but this development revolutionized trade in the region. The Central Asians became producers and exporters of a highly valuable commercial product. New cities appeared on the map and old Central Asian urban centers grew significantly.

After successful wars in Central Asia, the Sassanids turned most of their attention to the West. King Shapur I suffered a setback at the Battle of Resaena in 244 but recovered. His army captured the city of Antiochia in Syria in 253 and defeated the Roman army led by the Emperor Valerian (253–260) in the Battle of Edessa in 259. The Sassanids' fortunes turned a few decades later in the 270s and 280s, when under the rule of Bahram II (276–293) they experienced a series of defeats at the hands of Rome's Emperor Carus (282–283), followed by the further loss of several western provinces to the Roman emperor Diocletian (284–305). The wars on the western front ultimately exhausted the military power and economic resources of the Sassanids.

The Eurasian steppe from the fourth to seventh centuries A.D. also experienced significant changes. A combination of demographic, climatic and political factors forced numerous nomadic groups to move from southern Siberia and Altai to the Central Asian steppe and to cross the Syr Darya River into Transoxiana. The first large wave of ferocious nomadic armies confronted the Sassanids in Central Asia in the mid-fourth century. *Shah-n-Shah* Shapur II (ca. 309–379) mobilized his disciplined heavy and light cavalry squadrons and crushed the intruders, apparently extending Sassanid control to the east, all the way to the Jetysuu region. This decisive victory helped to pacify the Transoxiana for several decades. However, the Sassanids were not so successful in dealing with the second large wave of intrusions a century later. In the mid-fifth century new nomadic groups, the Hephthalites, moved into the Transoxiana. This time the war inflicted heavy casualties on the Sassanid army and was prolonged for several decades as the tides of fortune changed several times. In 484, during one of these campaigns, *Shah-n-Shah* Peroz I (?–484) was defeated and killed in battle along with his entire army.

There were victories. Under Kavadh (488–531), and especially under his son Khosrau I (531–579), the Sassanids again faced their most powerful enemy, the Roman Empire. They managed to successfully fight both the Eastern Roman Empire (which had split from the Roman Empire in 395 A.D.) and the Hephthalites.

However, in the early seventh century the Sassanid Empire again experienced a series of internal troubles and suffered defeats by the Romans. The state and its army were significantly weakened, and almost all Sassanid provinces were by this time impoverished by high taxes, neglect and mismanagement. In addition, the *Shah-n-Shah*s of these final days largely misread the changing geopolitical situation on their southwestern borders, where the Arab tribes, mobilized by the power of their new Islamic creed, were gaining strength (see map 15). The Sassanids were so much preoccupied by their internal affairs that they paid little attention to the Muslim Arabs who defeated all their rivals and gradually built a large and powerful state. In 637 the Muslims prepared to launch a series of military campaigns against the large Persian army, culminating with the Battle of al-Qadisiyyh. The Sassanid Empire never recovered from this defeat and began falling apart. It ended in 651 with the death of the last *Shah-n-Shah*, Yazdegerd III (?–651).

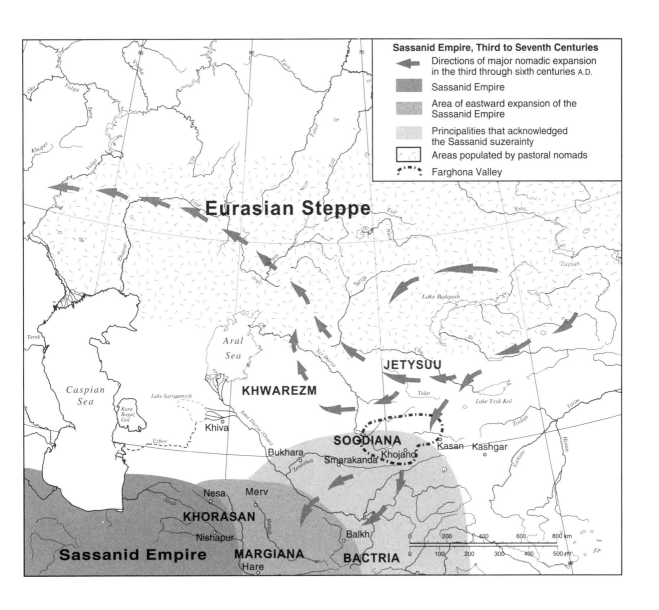

Sassanid Empire, Third to Seventh Centuries

Directions of major nomadic expansion in the third through sixth centuries A.D.

Sassanid Empire

Area of eastward expansion of the Sassanid Empire

Principalities that acknowledged the Sassanid suzerainty

Areas populated by pastoral nomads

Farghona Valley

Eurasian Steppe

Caspian Sea

Aral Sea

Lake Sarygamysh

Kara Bogaz Gol

Khiva

Lake Balqash

JETYSUU

Ili

Zaysan

Lake Ysyk Kol

Tarim

KHWAREZM

SOGDIANA

Bukhara

Smarakanda

Khojand

Kasan

Kashgar

Nesa

Merv

KHORASAN

Nishapur

MARGIANA

Hare

Balkh

BACTRIA

Sassanid Empire

Terek

Khoper

Volga

Oka

Sura

Ural

Tobol

Turu

Esil

Nura

Sarysu

Ertix

Chu

Talas

Toskan

Honan

Tarkunt

Zerafshan

Amu Darya (Oxus)

Uzboy

Syr Darya

Urgiz

Kara

Aral

Marghab

0   200   400   600   800 km

0 100 200 300 400 500 mi

Map 11: Early Turkic Empires

In the early sixth century A.D. a new and formidable power entered the political scenery of Central Asia—the Turks. A combination of various factors whose relative force and significance historians still vigorously debate—environmental changes, rapid population growth, pressure from neighboring tribes and the political intrigues of the Chinese Empire—forced the Turks to move around. Between the third and eighth centuries A.D. they formed a number of consecutive large migration waves reaching from their heartland in Southern Siberia all the way to China, Central Asia, the Middle East and Eastern Europe (Findley 2005).

Between the mid-fifth and mid-sixth centuries the Turks had engaged in a series of military conflicts with the competing tribal confederations of Jou-Jan (Rouran) and the Uigurs, who came from the area east of Jetysuu. These conflicts and external threats brought the Turkic peoples together and honed their military and strategic skills. In addition, they effectively strengthened their position by allowing various clans and tribes to join their confederation and enjoy equal rights. By the 520s the Turks had assembled a large army led by Bumin (also Tumin) Khaghan (?–ca.552), who began advancing to the east, the south and the west.

The political situations in both the south and in the west were favorable for Turkic expansion. In the south, the Chinese Empire and its rivals had been weakened by numerous long-lasting military conflicts and internal strife. To the west, the Hephthalites of Central Asia were exhausted after a series of wars with the Sassanids; the Sassanids in turn were weakened by their unceasing war with the eastern Roman Empire. In this environment Bumin defeated the Jou-Jan, the Uigurs and Oghuzs, and in 552 declared himself Il-Khaghan (King of Kings), but unexpectedly died.

Remarkably, his successors—his son Mughan Khaghan (ruled 553–572) and his brother Istemi (ruled 552–575)—swiftly consolidated joint power in their hands. Mughan Khaghan became supreme khaghan, controlling the territory of the Turkic heartland in the east, while Istemi became ruler of the western parts of the empire roughly congruent with the territory of Central Asia. This division would survive for the next millennium, with Central Asia often referred to as Western Turkistan and the eastward territory dubbed Eastern Turkistan. In the 550s the Turks shifted to the east and the south, establishing control over northern China. In the 560s they turned their attention to Central Asia. Around 563 the Turks defeated the Hephthalites and established control over the Tarim River Basin, Jetysuu, probably some parts of the Maveranahr and vast areas of the Central Asian steppe.

To what degree the Turks controlled the Central Asian urban centers and the exact nature of their relations with the settlers are not clear. Some sources indicate that these cities paid tributes and reparations to the Turkic khaghans, accepted Turkic garrisons and Turkic settlers and provided administrative and financial expertise to the Turks. In exchange, the Turks did not intervene in their internal affairs and provided protection to the caravan trade on the regional and international routes.

After the deaths of Mughan Khaghan (572) and Istemi (575), however, the situation changed dramatically. The Turkic Empire experienced its first major crisis. Differences and rivalries between the east and west wings of the empire became irreconcilable. By the 580s the Turkic Empire had split into an Eastern and Western Khanate. This development significantly weakened the powers of both. The strength of the Eastern Khanate was further undermined by its wars against numerous rebelling tribes and missteps in its intervention into a civil war in China. In 630 the Khaghan of the Eastern Khanate was defeated in battle and captured by the Chinese. Without its leader the Eastern Turkic tribal confederation disintegrated into small competing groups. Fortunes changed for a time in the late seventh century, when the Eastern Turks united once more under the leadership first of Kapagan Khaghan (ruled ca. 691–716) and then Bilge Khaghan (ruled ca. 716–734). With the death of Bilge Khaghan in 734 the khanate began a series of disastrous intertribal wars and ultimately ceased to exist in 745.

The Western Turkic Khanate experienced a broadly similar fate. In the 580s its leaders switched international alliances, joining the Byzantines against the Sassanids. The Turks gathered their army and crossed the Amu Darya River. However, they lost a decisive battle at Herat in 588. Under Tan Khaghan (ruled ca. 618–630) the Turks ventured from their bases in Jetysuu and eastern Maveranahr, all the way to the Caspian Sea and the Caucasus. This series of wars was costly. They were a major drain on resources and troops, yet they brought almost no rewards to the tribal leaders. The Sassanids skillfully exploited rising dissatisfaction in the Turkic army, and through various intrigues stirred mutiny, which led in 630 to Tan Khaghan's murder. His death was followed by nearly half a century of devastating intertribal wars. The Chinese seized the moment and moved against the Western Turkic tribes, who were defeated and ultimately vanquished from the political scene in the 740s.

Turkic domination of the Jetysuu, the Maveranahr, and the vast Eurasian steppe had far-reaching consequences for the whole region. It changed the ethnic composition and marked the beginning of a long era of interaction between Turks and Iranians that enriched both cultures. Turks' expansion had also pushed numerous smaller tribes across the Eurasian steppe all the way to Eastern Europe, Asia Minor and the Balkans.

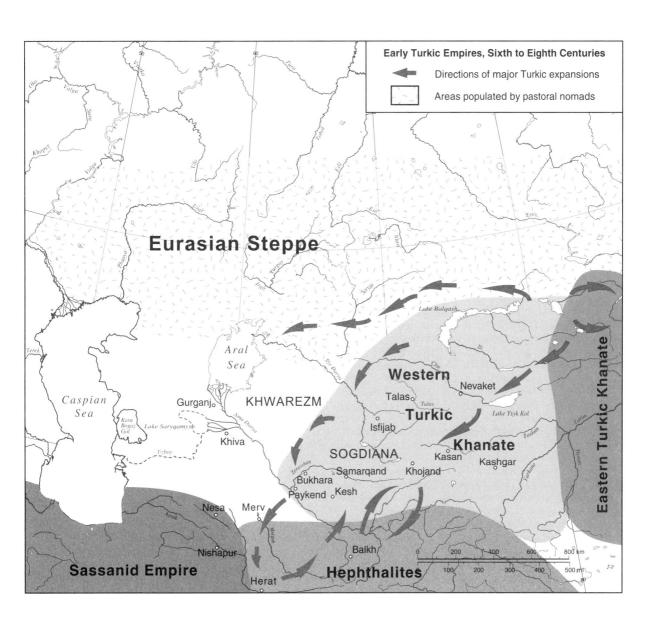

Early Turkic Empires, Sixth to Eighth Centuries

Directions of major Turkic expansions

Areas populated by pastoral nomads

Eurasian Steppe

Aral Sea

Caspian Sea

Kara Bogaz Gol

Lake Saryqamysh

Uzboy

Gurganj

KHWAREZM

Khiva

Western

Turkic

Khanate

Talas

Nevaket

Isfijab

Lake Ysyk Kol

SOGDIANA

Kasan

Kashgar

Khojand

Samarqand

Bukhara

Paykend

Kesh

Nesa

Merv

Balkh

Nishapur

Sassanid Empire

Herat

Hephthalites

Eastern Turkic Khanate

Lake Balqash

0   200   400   600   800 km

100   200   300   400   500 mi

Map 12: Religions in Central Asia: Zoroastrianism, Buddhism and Christianity

Religious beliefs were highly significant, and in some cases crucial, in the development of ancient civilizations everywhere, as well as in the ways that different empires, states and peoples interacted. Central Asia was no exception. Religious development between the sixth century B.C. and sixth century A.D. played an important role in the cultural and political changes. What made this region different from other places in the world, however, was the intensity of interfaith interactions (Foltz 1999). Several factors worked in unique combination: large-scale migration; active trade; multiethnic composition of major urban and rural areas; and fierce competition between various missionary groups for proselytizing advantage. The geographical position of Central Asia at the crossroads of major cultural highways also contributed to this intensity.

Although it is very difficult to reconstruct the earliest religious traditions of Central Asia, a significant body of archeological artifacts and some written and oral sources lead us to believe that the early Central Asians practiced various forms of polytheism. In settled areas the religious traditions were served by influential groups of professional priests. In the tribal nomadic and seminomadic areas, religious needs were probably served by shamans and wandering missionaries.

The popular beliefs of the Eurasian Steppe. The popular beliefs that dominated the Central Eurasian steppe for thousands of years probably survived in the pre-Islamic religious practices of the Turkic-speaking nomadic people. Their pantheon included a main god who controlled the heavenly universe and his rival who controlled the underworld. Both were served by numerous lesser gods. At the center of this belief system was the god of blue sky, Tengri (Tenri), the most powerful and mighty master of the forces of nature. Next to him was the goddess Umai (Umay), symbol of the earth, motherhood and fertility. There was also the god of the underworld, Erglig, who guarded the world of the dead and hunted for people's souls. Many nomads also believed in totems, sacred animals that played a role in the tribe's earliest beginnings. The wolf, for example, was regarded by many as a totem-protector of all Turkic tribes. In addition, people worshiped numerous local spirits, saints and patrons.

Zoroastrianism. Zoroastrianism was founded by Zoroaster who began preaching the revelation he claimed to have received from the "Wise Lord" (*Ahura Mazda*) probably in the sixth century B.C. His teaching came to be systematically presented as the sacred scripture known as the *Avesta*. Zoroaster preached the oneness of God, who is served by a retinue of assistants distantly resembling, in form and role, the Judeo-Christian archangels, and who is challenged by Evil (*Ahriman* in Persian). Humans have freedom to choose between right (Truth) and wrong (Lies). Upon death, Zoroaster taught, each person's soul is taken to the Bridge of Discrimination and judged as to their fitness to enter paradise or to fall into hell. In Zoroastrianism, fire symbolized Ahura Mazda's power, presence and purity, and therefore sacred fires had to be maintained in every Zoroastrian temple. Some scholars believe that Zoroaster began preaching in Khwarezm (now Uzbekistan) and his teaching gradually spread to Bactria, Sogdiana, Khorasan and many other areas in Central Asia and along the Great Silk Road. Over time it expanded all over the Persian world, where it was the dominant religion for several centuries.

Buddhism. Buddhism arrived in Central Asia in the fifth century B.C. A popular legend claims that the Buddha—Siddhartha Gautama (ca. 563–483 B.C.)—who lived and taught in the region of modern northern India, Pakistan and Afghanistan, met merchants from Central Asia and conveyed to them his teachings. Gautama's title, "Buddha," is translated as "awakened" or "enlightened." His followers systematized his teachings in sacred writings called the Three Baskets (*Tipitaka*), covering the three main dimensions of his teaching: the practice of Buddhism at its highest level; the lessons and sayings of the Buddha; and cosmology and theology. These teachings place human nature within never-ending cycles of birth, life and death, in which an individual's actions affect his next rebirth. Populations of Central Asia's settled areas and the nomads of the steppe both experienced the influence of Buddhism to a significant degree. Moreover, Buddhism dominated in the oases of Afghanistan and western China (eastern Turkistan) before the arrival of Islam.

Christianity. The followers of the so-called Nestorian school of Christianity began arriving in large numbers in Central Asia in the fifth and sixth centuries A.D. Nestorius (ca. 386–451 A.D.), the patriarch of Constantinople (now Istanbul), came into conflict with the Catholic Church in the mid-fifth century over doctrinal differences on a number of key theological issues. The Council of Ephesus condemned Nestorius and his supporters and exiled them from Constantinople. To escape persecution the Nestorians fled to Persia, India, Central Asia and as far as Mongolia and China. They established large churches and monasteries in Samarqand, Kashgar and Chang'an (modern Xi'an), and exercised significant influence in the courts of Chinese emperors and some nomadic empires (for example, Uigurs and Mongols).

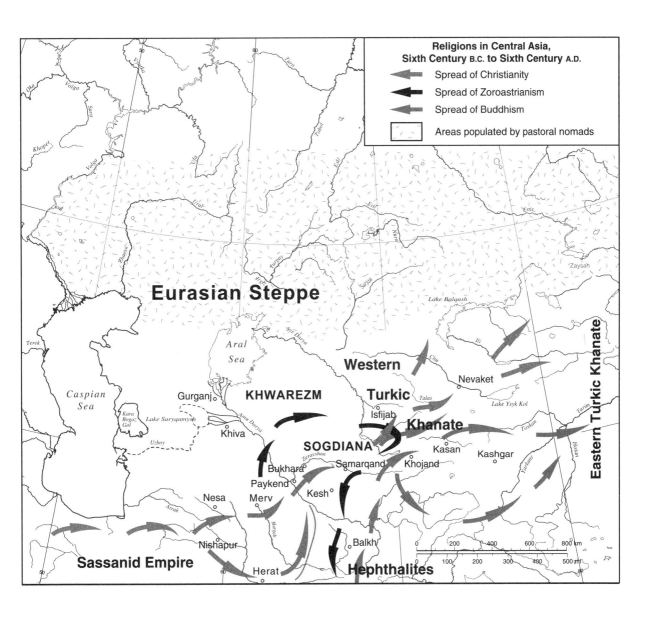

Religions in Central Asia,
Sixth Century B.C. to Sixth Century A.D.

→ Spread of Christianity

→ Spread of Zoroastrianism

→ Spread of Buddhism

Areas populated by pastoral nomads

Oka

Volga

Sura

Khopet

Terek

Caspian
Sea

*Kara
Bogaz
Gol*

Zhavya

Volga

Ufa

Ural

Aral
Sea

Lake Saryqamysh

Uzboy

Gurganj

Khiva

KHWAREZM

Amu Darya

Eurasian Steppe

Turu

Tobol

Esil

Tura

Irtish

Zaysan

Lake Balqash

Ertis

Ili

Nevaket

Western

Turkic

Chu

Talas

Isfijab

Khanate

Lake Ysyk Kol

Toskan

Kashgar

Yarkanf

Houan

Eastern Turkic Khanate

SOGDIANA

Zeravshan

Bukhara

Paykend

Merv

Nesa

Atrak

Murgab

Nishapur

Herat

Sassanid Empire

Samarqand

Kesh

Kasan

Khojand

Balkh

Hephthalites

0   200   400   600   800 km

0   100   200   300   400   500 mi

Map 13: International Trade and the Beginning of the Great Silk Road

From the earliest ancient times the states in and around Central Asia increasingly engaged in trade and in technological, cultural, political and dynastic exchanges. Very often these contacts started with gift exchanges or interdynastic marriages between rulers of neighboring states; they later extended to political alliances and commercial operations. Increasing specialization among the animal herders, settled farmers and craftsmen boosted productivity and stimulated barter exchange and trade at various levels. These developments led, as early as the sixth century B.C. to the consolidation of local and regional markets, and to the extension of neighborhood bazaars where local people freely bartered and traded various goods and products.

The growth in trade was stimulated by innovative developments in transportation and finance. By the sixth century B.C. the local people had greatly improved their transportation capacity as caravans increased in size. The selective breeding process helped to adapt domestic animals—Bactrian camels, horses and bulls—for carrying goods longer distances, and improvements in transportation technology helped to establish and expand the trade routes. At the same time, local rulers established more or less clear norms for issuing their currencies, while local dealers developed a rudimentary international currency market.

These changes in turn facilitated the establishment of a commercial-scale transportation and trade infrastructure for the era's local, regional and international trade. Of course, the economic, political and legal changes and technological advances also contributed to the rise of this trade. Tradable items included highly prized nephrite jade and race and cavalry horses that were exported to China, and silk, porcelain and many other exotic goods sent from China to Central Asia, Persia, the Roman Empire and the rest of the Mediterranean and Egypt. High-quality weapons were traded in all directions.

Regional and international trade became increasingly profitable, supported by the growth of wholesale stores at the bazaars. With the rise of the trade capitals, and consequently the rise of the trading missions (caravans), there was serious demand for caravanserais, inns, that provided safe accommodation for travelers. From the early days merchants also nurtured positive relations with and patronage from local rulers by frequently supplying exotic and luxury gifts. This gift-giving tradition gradually evolved into regular and more-or-less clearly defined taxes. In the end, the local rulers found they had substantial motive to provide legal, military and financial guaranties to the merchants.

Some ancient rulers went even further by establishing, protecting and operating strategically important highways. One such road was known as the Persian Royal Road. It was probably established in the fifth century B.C., and it stretched 2,000 miles (about 3,200 kilometers), connecting Persian-controlled seaports on the eastern Mediterranean with trading and political centers on the Tigris River. This road was serviced by caravanserais, postal stations and small military garrisons. Similar but probably less sophisticated roads connected Persia with the ancient cities of Merv, Bukhara, Samarqand, Herat and other centers.

Eventually the many fragmented trade routes expanded far enough to connect the major trading centers in China, Central Asia, Persia, Mesopotamia and the Mediterranean. Many scholars date the beginning of the Great Silk Road to the second century B.C. During this period the rulers of the Han Dynasty (ca. 206 B.C.–220 A.D.) discovered commercially viable routes to Central Asia, Persia and Europe.

Geographical and climatic considerations imposed significant limitations on the direction of the trade routes. The high and inhospitable mountains of the Tian Shan, Pamirs and Himalayas created serious obstacles for trade between the richest and most advanced ancient civilizations of China, Persia and the Mediterranean.

Ancient travelers had two choices. One was to go through the passes in the Tian-Shan and the Pamirs Mountains: Anxi, Khotan, Yarkend, Kashgar, Balkh and Merv, and then to Persia and the Mediterranean. The other was to travel through the broad stretches of grassland to the north of the mountain slopes: Anxi, Turfan, Urumchi, Balasagun, Chach (Tashkent), Samarqand, Bukhara, Merv and on, once again, to Persia and the Mediterranean. Of course, at different times varying circumstances could cause the routes to deviate significantly.

The Silk Road developed its own business cycles, as it was greatly affected by the political, military and economic development in all regions along its length: in China, in the principalities of Central Asia, the nomadic states and empires of the Eurasian Steppe, in Persia and the Mediterranean world. Large-scale trade flourished along the transcontinental Silk Road for about 400 years until its collapse in the early second century A.D. due to the disintegration of both the Han Empire in China and the Parthian Empire in Central Asia, and the beginning of the "great population movement" in the steppe zone between Mongolia and the Black Sea. The Silk Road was reinvented between the seventh and tenth centuries A.D. under the Tang Dynasty (618–907 A.D.) and again between the thirteenth and fifteenth centuries (under the protection of the Mongol Empire).

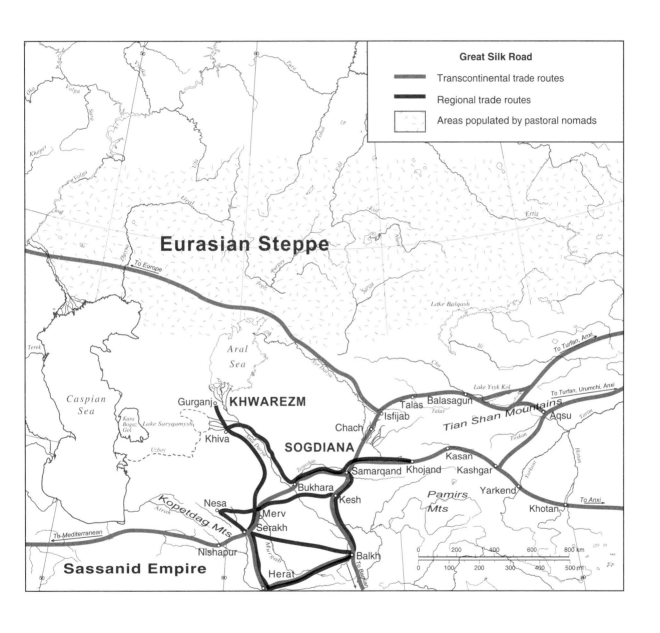

Great Silk Road

— Transcontinental trade routes

— Regional trade routes

Areas populated by pastoral nomads

Khopet

Volga

Oka

Sura

Ufa

Ural

Tobol

Iset

Tara

Ertis

Eurasian Steppe

Zhayyq

To Europe

Emil

Nura

Terek

Terek

Lake Balqash

Ili

Aral Sea

Caspian Sea

Kara Bogaz Gol

Lake Saryqamysh

Uzboy

Gurganj

KHWAREZM

Khiva

Syr Darya

Chach

Isfijab

Talas

Balasagun

Talas

Lake Ysyk Kol

Chu

To Turfan, Anxi

To Turfan, Urumchi, Anxi

Tian Shan Mountains

Aqsu

Tarim

SOGDIANA

Amu Darya

Zerayshan

Samarqand

Khojand

Kasan

Kashgar

Toxkan

Bukhara

Kesh

Pamirs Mts

Yarkend

Yarkant

Hotian

Nesa

Atrak

Kopetdag Mts

Merv

Serakh

Murgab

Khotan

To Anxi

To Mediterranean

Nishapur

To Bamian

Balkh

Herat

Sassanid Empire

| 0 | 200 | 400 | 600 | 800 km |

| 0 | 100 | 200 | 300 | 400 | 500 mi |

III

Islamic Golden Age, Seventh to Twelfth Centuries A.D.

Map 14: The Political Map of Central Asia in the Middle Ages

The beginning of the Middle Ages in Central Asia in some degree resembled the development of Western Europe. In Europe, the arrival of the medieval era followed several dramatic events and changes: the pillage of Rome in 410 A.D. and the subsequent collapse of trade, manufacturing and Roman central administration; dramatic cultural and population changes (including the arrival of tribes from Central Asia); and changes in the religious landscape. In Central Asia the beginning of the new era was similarly marked by the collapse of the major power, the Sassanid Empire, in 651 (see map 10); dramatic population change; changes in the religious landscape—in this case the rapid spread of Islam in the region in the eighth century; and a temporary collapse of trade. There was one very important difference: in Europe the beginning of the Middle Ages also signaled the arrival of feudalism, a system based centrally on ownership of the land (the *feud*, or fief) as the currency of power, and on the social, economic and political relationship between the various ranks of landowners (the nobles), their tenants (knights or vassals) and the unfree, landless peasant or serf class. In Central Asia in the Middle Ages, however, feudalism and clear-cut changes in either political or economic relations are not so evident.

The Central Asian region entered the Middle Ages in the seventh century (some scholars date its beginning as the sixth), with political fragmentation and instability. In the seventh century the great powers—the Sassanids, Chinese and Turks—were strong enough to raid the cities and oases of Central Asia to demand reparations and tributes, but they were too weak to maintain full political control of the region, establish effective administration or revive trade. For about a century between the mid-sixth and mid-seventh centuries, regional and international trade stagnated. The economy of Central Asia, especially its manufacturing sector and commercial services, declined, leading to a significant drop in living standards in the region. The geopolitical situation in Central Asia changed significantly during the Middle Ages and ultimately affected development in the region. Four international forces were significant in this process.

One of the most important changes was the gradual weakening and eventual collapse of the Sassanid Empire. Between 500 and 651 the Sassanids overstretched their economic and military resources by fighting wars on three fronts simultaneously: in the west against their archenemy, the Byzantine Empire; in the east to check the rising power of various mini-kingdoms in the region that became known as Tokharistan and in Central Asia; and in the northeast in bloody conflicts with the Western Turkic Khanate.

During this era the Chinese Empire quickly rose in international prominence after the establishment of the Tang Dynasty (618–907 A.D.). The Tang emperors conducted administrative and military reforms, put an end to destructive civil wars and revived military might. In 630 they defeated the Western Turkic Khanate and captured Ton Ynghu Khaghan. By the mid-seventh century the Chinese had established control in the Tarim River basin. By the late seventh century they had expanded their influence over a number of oases in the Jetysuu and Maveranahr.

Between the fifth and seventh centuries the Roman Empire—another long-time partner and an important player in Central Asian political and economic development—fragmented and significantly declined in importance, and along with it the Mediterranean economic system. The almost constant warfare between the eastern Roman Empire and the Sassanids had sapped their wealth and prosperity. There was little to no demand for luxury goods and trade from China and Central Asia, though the eastern Roman Empire and Turkic khanates continued to exchange regular diplomatic missions.

Between 550 and 651 the Turks were consumed by perpetual internecine wars. Their populations were burdened by the constant recruitment of ordinary herders for the numerous military campaigns that yielded few economic gains for ordinary tribesmen. That many tribes regularly revolted against their ambitious leaders or joined groups who challenged the powers of the Turkic dynasties is not surprising. In retribution, the Turkic armies often massacred members of unruly or opposing tribes, or pushed them into the West or East, further undermining their own power base.

During this era the Central Asian principalities remained on the periphery of the great powers, yet the region was still viewed as an important geopolitical asset by many. Control over and alliances with the Central Asian states could help to gain comparative advantage over opponents. Reparations and tributes from the area could finance costly military campaigns, and trade with the region could help to gain new markets for goods, including goods of military importance such as horses for the cavalry.

In this environment of instability and political chaos a new power emerged on the outskirts of the Sassanid Empire. The Arabs and their Muslim allies would come to play a decisive role in the development of the Middle East, Persia and Central Asia for many centuries.

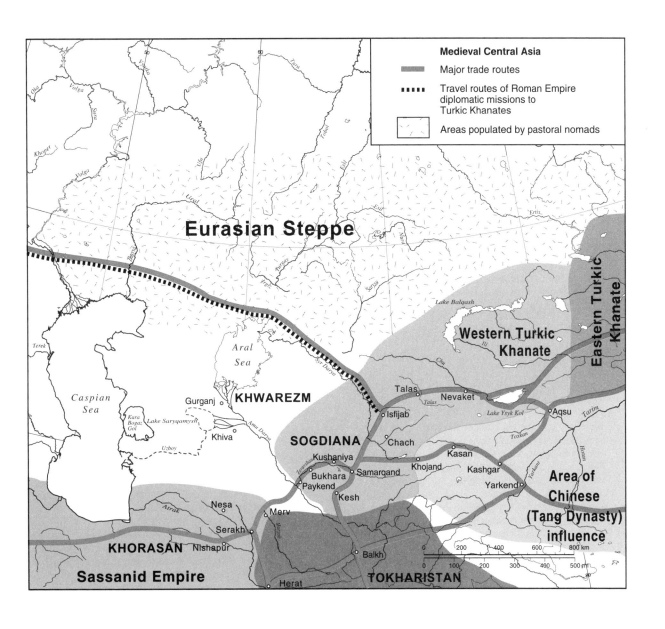

Map 15: The Arab Conquest of Central Asia

Numerous competing Arab and non-Arab tribes were brought together by the skillful politics and universal appeal of Muhammad (ca. 570–632). In 610 he declared that he had experienced a series of revelations and gradually began gathering followers (Muslims). Despite an early setback in 622, when he and his followers were forced to escape from Mecca to Medina, he triumphantly returned to Mecca in 630, establishing the city as the center of the Islamic state. Islam soon became the dominant religion among most Arabs.

After Muhammad's death in 632, the leadership of the Islamic world was transferred to caliphs who assumed supreme spiritual and political authority in the Muslim state. The earliest Muslim state under the first four caliphs (632–661) was formed under a single, straightforward mandate: the spread of Islam to all corners of the world. Several factors contributed to its strength: its call for social justice, regardless of race, color, social background, tribal origin or language; its enforcement of law and order; and its support for trade. In the military sphere, the Muslims introduced an effective combination of compact professional units and massive volunteer armies, and efficiently used cavalry and infantry.

Under the leadership of the first four caliphs, the Muslim armies achieved significant success in crushing the Sassanid forces. They captured Damascus in 635, Ctesiphon in 636, Jerusalem in 638, and Nehavend in 642. They finally defeated the last *Shah-n-Shah* of the Sassanid Empire in series of battles. The last *Shah-n-Shah* was killed in 651 before the Central Asian city of Merv (Gibb 1923, rep. 1970). The Arab commanders made Merv their base of further operations in the region, raiding Herat in 651 and Balkh (Bactra) in 652, though the first raids in Khwarezm did not bring any decisive success. In 675–676 the Arabs battled the rulers of Bukhara, Samarqand and Termez (Tarmita). In 680–681 they campaigned in Maveranahr, again asserting their control over Bukhara and Samarqand, and attempting to capture the city of Khojand farther east in the Farghona Valley. Internal instability in the late seventh century forced them to halt their activities in Central Asia, though a small Arab garrison was established at a base in Termez and maintained semi-independent status between 690 and 704.

In the early eighth century the Muslim armies continued their campaigns in the region, but the nature of those campaigns changed significantly. In the first place, around this time the composition of the armies was transformed from a predominantly Arab into a truly multiethnic force, as the Arab commanders welcomed Muslim converts into their ranks. Many of the converts were Persians or belonged to various tribes and groups with kinship or cultural links to the Central Asian communities. Secondly, the Muslims attempted to establish a permanent presence in the region, rather than simply taking tributes and leaving. In 706 a Muslim army under the leadership of the highly capable commander Qutayba bin Muslim (?–715) crossed the Amu Darya River. One by one his army captured such important Central Asian urban centers as Paykend in 706, Bukhara in 709, Nakhsheb and Kesh in 710, and Samarqand in 712. He then turned eastward, capturing several important centers such as Chach (Tashkent) in 713 and Khojand in 715. Political developments in the caliphate soon intruded into the military affairs of the region. Qutayba refused to pledge an oath of fidelity to the new caliph, Sulayman ibn Abd al-Malik (ruled 715–717) and was killed. His troops immediately withdrew from the region.

The resulting power vacuum plunged the Central Asian cities into a succession of rebellions against Muslim governors for nearly three decades. Numerous incursions by Turkic armies and groups added to the misery and chaos in the region. By the 740s the internecine wars had taken their toll and the Turkic khanates were in a state of collapse. In this environment the Chinese armies saw an opportunity, and marched from Kashgar to Chach to capture the city. Their move toward Central Asia brought them into conflict with the growing Muslim interests in the region.

The decisive battle between the Chinese army, led by General Gao Xianzhi, and General Ziyad ibn Salih's Arab-Persian army took place in 751 on the Talas River, in the Jetysuu area. This was in fact one of the most important battles in the history of Central Asia (Bartold 1995), as its outcome would determine which power controlled the region. Each side brought an army approximately 100,000 strong, and the fighting was fierce. Both the Chinese and Muslims claimed victory, though for either it would probably have been Pyrrhic. The Chinese had to retreat to their military base in the Tarim River basin and Kashgar. The Muslims were unable to move beyond the Jetysuu area, though they remained in Central Asia.

One hundred years of Muslim presence in Central Asia, from the battle against the Sassanid *Shah-n-Shah* before the walls of Merv in 651 to the Battle of Talas in 751, significantly changed the geopolitical and cultural landscapes in the region. Central Asian economies were firmly linked to the economy of the Muslim caliphate as commercial relations and trade grew extensively.

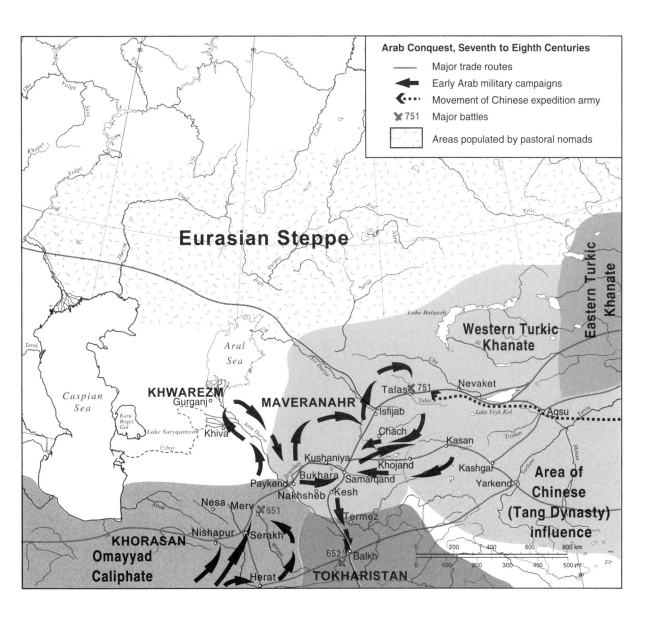

Arab Conquest, Seventh to Eighth Centuries

— Major trade routes

◄ Early Arab military campaigns

◄··· Movement of Chinese expedition army

✖751 Major battles

Areas populated by pastoral nomads

Ob

Volga

Khoper

Volga

Sura

Ura

Zhayk

Tobol

Irgiz

Torgay

Turgay

Isil

Tobol

Sarysu

Ertis

Eurasian Steppe

Terek

Caspian Sea

Aral Sea

Lake Balqash

Western Turkic Khanate

Eastern Turkic Khanate

Kara Boga: Gol

Lake Saryqamysh

Uzboy

KHWAREZM

Gurganj

Khiva

Amu Darya

MAVERANAHR

Syr Darya

Talas

Talas

✖751

Isfijab

Chach

Nevaket

Chu

Lake Ysyk Kol

Aqsu

Tarim

Kushaniya

Zeravshan

Bukhara

Paykend

Nakhsheb

Kesh

Samarqand

Khojand

Kasan

Toskan

Kashgar

Yarkend

Yarkant

Hotun

Area of Chinese (Tang Dynasty) influence

Nesa

Merv

✖651

Termez

Arak

Nishapur

Serakh

Murgab

652

✖

Balkh

KHORASAN Omayyad Caliphate

Herat

TOKHARISTAN

0   200   400   600   800 km

0   100   200   300   400   500 mi

Map 16: Consolidation of the Caliphate's Political Influence

The period from 751 onward became an era of further strengthening of the Islamic caliphate's position and Islamic influence in Central Asia. This era coincided with the demise of the Umayyad Caliphate (661–750) and the end of the civil war. The new Abbasid Dynasty (750–1258) quickly consolidated its political power by decisively moving against the various competing political groups and reforming the political and administrative systems of the Islamic Empire. Caliph Abu Jabar al-Mansur (ruled 754–775) paid significant attention to development in the eastern provinces. In a symbolic gesture he moved his capital from Damascus to Baghdad in 762. In an earlier move al-Mansur invited Abu Muslim, then the governor of Khorasan and Maveranahr, to his palace and ordered his execution in 755.

The power struggle in the caliphate and especially the death of Abu Muslim created a power vacuum in Central Asia. In addition, representatives of various revisionist and heretical groups in Islam, after losing battles, began moving into the empire's periphery, further disturbing the situation in Maveranahr and the eastern parts of Khorasan. Various political, social and non-Islamic religious groups also attempted to seize the moment and recapture political power in parts of the region. They became increasingly active in the face of the mass destruction of the Zoroastrian temples and sacred places.

One of the first uprisings occurred in 755, when supporters and loyalists of Abu Muslim rebelled. They were joined by those who strongly opposed Abbasid rule and their interpretation of Islam, as well as by some groups of Zoroastrians and representatives of the communalistic movement, the Hurramits. The rebels, under Sumbad Mag (some sources indicate that he was a Zoroastrian), managed to establish control over some rural areas of Khorasan. However, regular troops sent by the new Khorasan governor crushed the rebel militia and reestablished central authority in the region.

An uprising by another leader, Hashim al-Muqunna (ca. 775–780) represented a more serious threat to the political power of the caliphate in Maveranahr. Some sources claim that he was influenced by the teachings of Mazdakism (a communalist, populist ideology established in Persia in the sixth century). Al-Muqunna received considerable support from the rural population in Maveranahr and by 776 had established a power base on the outskirts of Bukhara. The al-Muqunna movement spread over large areas in Maveranahr, from Bukhara to Samarqand and Kesh. In late 776, however, the rebel army was defeated by regular troops sent by Bukhara's ruler. Al-Muqunna managed to escape and captured Samarqand, which he maintained control over for about a year, successfully fighting off regular armies sent from Bukhara and Merv. The rebel army then lost a series of battles in 778 and disintegrated into a guerrilla movement that retreated south from Samarqand, establishing bases in the mountains around the city of Kesh. It took the Khorasan ruler about two years to conquer all the strongholds, killing the rebels including al-Muqunna.

Another significant uprising took place in Samarqand between 806 and 810. Rebels led by Rafi ibn Leisa killed the provincial governor and attempted to extend their influence to the cities of Bukhara, Khojand and others. When disagreements within the ranks of the rebels weakened their position, the uprising was subdued by troops from Khorasan.

The series of large and small uprisings that inflamed the region between the 750s and early 800s had serious consequences for politics and religion in Central Asian society. As the governing troops crushed rebellion after rebellion, they eliminated the indigenous Central Asian elite, destroyed temples and shrines of various non-Islamic religious groups and forced a large number of Buddhist, Manichean and Zoroastrian clergy to move farther into the lands of the East, where they attempted to establish roots and influence, and achieved notable results. For example, the Uigur Khaghan Bogu (ruled ca. 759–779) was converted to Manichaeism and declared it the official religion of the khanate in 762. At the same time, the Buddhist communities were expanding their influence both in eastern Turkistan and in Tibet, where they achieved the status of official religion in about 787.

In Maveranahr, in contrast, a large number of Central Asians, especially among the urban elite, began accepting Islam and benefited from the strong and comprehensive Islamic educational system in the region. Administrative and educational reforms brought the Arab language and script into the region and gradually it became the language of government, law, science and art. Importantly, a growing number of Central Asian educated elite began traveling across the caliphate to enter into public administration, senior army ranks, clergy, the educational establishment and artistic communities. Central Asia increasingly became part of the Islamic world. The caliphate came to rely heavily on the local elite to maintain its political influence and control over the region.

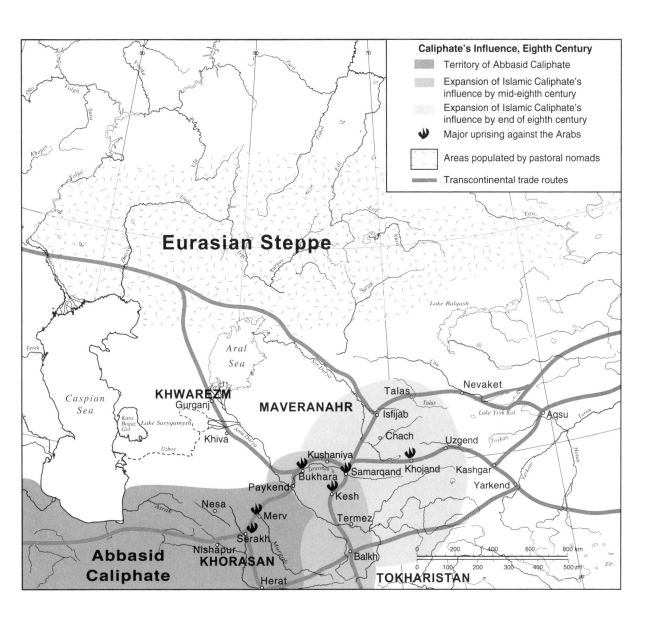

Caliphate's Influence, Eighth Century

- Territory of Abbasid Caliphate
- Expansion of Islamic Caliphate's influence by mid-eighth century
- Expansion of Islamic Caliphate's influence by end of eighth century
- Major uprising against the Arabs
- Areas populated by pastoral nomads
- Transcontinental trade routes

Eurasian Steppe

Oki
Volga
Sura
Khoper
Volga
Terek

Caspian Sea

Aral Sea

Kara Bogaz Gol
Lake Saryqamysh
Uzboy

KHWAREZM
Gurganj
Khiva

Ufa
Uil
Zhayyq
Irgiz
Torgay
Esil
Tobol
Esil
Nura
Sarysu

Lake Balqash

Ertis

Ili

MAVERANAHR

Talas
Talas
Isfijab
Chach

Nevaket

Lake Ysyk Kol
Aqsu
Tarim

Chu

Kushaniya
Zeravshan
Bukhara
Paykend
Samarqand
Khojand
Uzgend
Kashgar
Yarkend
Toxkan
Hotan
Yarkent

Kesh

Nesa
Merv
Termez
Serakh
Murgab
Nishapur
KHORASAN
Herat
Balkh

TOKHARISTAN

Abbasid Caliphate

0 200 400 600 800 km
0 100 200 300 400 500 mi

Map 17: The Samanids (875–999)

During the ninth century although Central Asia remained part of the caliphate with the Arabs playing an important role, the rulers of the Islamic Empire increasingly relied on local elites for governing and administration. In this environment several local families and clans rose to prominence. Gradually they acquired a significant degree of autonomy from the caliph and began building their own political bases in the region. From those clans rose the dynasties of the Tahirids, Saffarids, Samanids and various others (Gafurov 2005). In the end, the Samanids emerged ascendant, founding of one of the first Iranian Islamic dynasties.

The dynasty's founder, Saman Khuda, came from a prominent family of landlords, probably from the area between Samarqand and Termez. He sent his grandsons to serve at the court of the Khorasan governor and eventually they were appointed to administer Farghona, Chach and Herat. They demonstrated potent administrative and diplomatic skills. In 875 the caliph appointed one of the members of the clan, Nasr Saman (ruled 875–892), governor of Samarqand. From there Nasr Saman also administered the whole of Maveranahr. This date is traditionally perceived as the beginning of the Samanid dynasty and state.

Nasr Saman faced considerable challenges during his reign. His numerous brothers, uncles and nephews, while nominally accepting him as senior among equals, in fact ignored him. It took prodigious diplomatic maneuvering over a long period for Nasr to avoid war against all those family members. After Nasr's death in 892, his brother Ismail (ruled 892–907) declared himself ruler of Maveranahr and moved the capital to Bukhara. Ismail proved to be a skillful commander and diplomat, fighting off all other contenders, including those supported by the caliph. He consolidated his political control all over the region and built up an effective administration and army. In order to strengthen their legitimacy and appeal to local elites, the Samanids declared that their clan descended from the Sassanid emperor Bahram Chobin.

Ismail paid particular attention to reforming and building redoubtable armed forces. One of his innovations was the mass recruitment of Turkic warriors into his cavalry units. In 893 his army captured the cities of Taraz and Otrar in the far northeastern corner of the state, making them key military outposts in the fight against the Turkic nomadic confederations and important centers of Islamic learning in the Turkic lands. In 900 he successfully fought off an invasion by the Saffarids from their base in northern Khorasan, defeating them in a decisive battle before the city of Balkh.

Then in 900 and 901 he annexed two remote southern provinces east of the Caspian Sea. He also managed to extend his control to the Sogdiana and Herat.

Under Nasr II Samanid (ruled 914–943), the Samanid Empire reached its peak. The dynasty reigned over all the lands from the Caspian Sea in the west to the Farghona and Jetysuu valleys in the east, and their influence reached to Khwarezm in the north and Herat in the south, with the rulers of those centers becoming vassals. The Samanids spent lavishly on the building of military fortresses, mosques, palaces, caravanserais and various public buildings. They also supported the arts and sciences, and sponsored numerous scholars who worked at the Samanid court. The political stabilization of extensive territory in Maveranahr and eastern Khorasan brought significant economic growth and prosperity, stimulating the expansion of local, regional and international trade as well as mining—especially of silver, gold, jade—in the Farghona valley, Zeravshan River and other areas. However, the Samanids' most important impact was in the religious area, by spreading Islam through intensive missionary work among the various Turkic tribes within the empire. Many scholars trace the Turkic tribes' enduring mass acceptance of Islam to the Samanid era.

Nevertheless, in the tenth century the Samanids began facing serious challenges and rivalries. In midcentury the political stability and cohesiveness of the regime was undermined by the deep rivalry between two theological schools in Islam, the Sunnis (the traditional Islamic school) and the Ismailis (a group close to the Shi'a interpretation of Islam). The Sunni school won out and inspired purges of Ismaili followers throughout the state, including from the ranks of the army. The Ismaili were driven underground but continued their work in all major cities and towns across the region. From 947 to 954 serious internal strife within the Samanid family provoked a series of military conflicts. This was followed by revolts of local rulers and army generals. In addition, from 990 to 992 the Turkic armies entered the Jetysuu area and marched to its capital, Bukhara. Only the sudden death of their khan obliged them to withdraw. The Samanid Empire never recovered from these cataclysms and began to crumble.

The last Samanid rulers inherited a very weak kingdom under constant attack from their powerful neighbors to the south and north. In 999 the Karakhanid Turks gathered a large army in Jetysuu and invaded Maveranahr. They captured Bukhara and imprisoned the entire ruling family. The Samanid kingdom disappeared from the political map and a new dynasty established its power in the region—the Karakhanids.

Samanid Dynasty, 875–999

Territory of Samanids

Territorial expansions of Samanids at the peak of their power

Farghona Valley

Areas populated by pastoral nomads

Eurasian Steppe

KARAKHANIDS

JETYSUU

KHWAREZM

MAVERANAHR

Caspian Sea

Aral Sea

Nevaket

Farab (Otrar)

Talas (Taraz)

Isfijab

Chach

Kushaniya

Bukhara

Samarqand

Khojand

Uzgend

Kashgar

Yarkend

Aqsu

Lake Ysyk Kol

Paykend

Kesh

Gurganj

Khiva

Nesa

Merv

Serakh

Termez

Gorgan

Nishapur

Balkh

900

Herat

KHORASAN

Kara Bogaz Gol

Lake Saryqamysh

Uzboy

Aral Sea

Volga

Oka

Sura

Volga

Zhiguy

Khopet

Terek

Atrak

Amu Darya

Syr Darya

Zeravshan

Murgab

Ufa

Irgiz

Fargoi

Tobol

Esil

Nura

Saryu

Esil

Ishim

Ili

Chu

Talas

Foxkan

Tarim

Holein

Yarkanr

Lake Balqash

Ertix

50

60

70

50

0   200   400   600   800 km

0   100   200   300   400   500 mi

Map 18: The Karakhanid State (999–1140)

In the ninth and tenth centuries the descendants of the early Turkic empires began gathering strength again in the areas between Mongolia and Jetysuu. By the late ninth century they felt themselves strong enough to enter the political scene and to challenge the power of the Samanids at the prosperous Maveranahr oases. This time, however, the Turks entered Central Asia under very different circumstances and in a very different environment. By the tenth century, they had firmly established themselves on the eastern and northern borders of the Samanid Empire, including the areas around the Syr Darya river basin and the Aral Sea.

The Karakhanid tribal confederation emerged in the mid-tenth century with its center in eastern Turkistan. In 992 the supreme ruler (*bogra khan*) led his troops in a war against the Samanids and captured their capital, Bukhara. However, his sudden death forced the army to retreat to the Jetysuu area. A new *bogra khan*, Ahmad Arslan Qara Khan (ruled ca. 998–1017) invaded the Samanid state again. This time he defeated the Samanid army, capturing Bukhara in 999. Most scholars consider that year the beginning of the Karakhanid Empire. This empire at its zenith controlled the territory of Maveranahr, Jetysuu and parts of eastern Turkistan.

The Karakhanid rulers maintained their stronghold in the eastern parts of Central Asia, in the cities of Balasagun and Kashgar. Within a few decades these cities grew into bustling urban centers of about 100,000 inhabitants, hosting numerous mosques, Christian churches and probably monasteries and Islamic *madrasas*. The supreme ruler of the empire possessed significant power and military potential. He was able to mobilize an army of between 100,000 and 150,000 men at the first call, and he probably had a steady inflow of revenues from taxing trade, industry and farming. This income funded numerous public construction works in the capital and in major cities across the state. Politically, however, the state remained a loose confederation of tribal rulers. The Karakhanid era signifies important changes in Turkic culture, including the formation of Muslim Turkic identity and the codification of the Turkic cultural legacy in the 1070s (Kashgari 1982).

From its beginning, the Karakhanid state was politically quite unstable, as various individuals and clans vigorously fought for power and influence. At the same time, the Karakhanids faced formidable threats from the south, where the Ghaznavid dynasty rose to prominence, establishing its center in the city of Ghazna (in present-day Afghanistan). In 1008 the Karakhanids lost an important battle before the city of Balkh that halted their expansion south of the Amu Darya River. In another setback, they lost influence over the Khwarezm, as the Ghazna ruler captured the capital of Khwarezm

(Gurganj) in 1017 and installed a governor hostile to the Karakhanids. During the reign of Usuf Kadyr-Khan (ruled ca. 1026–1032) and his son Suleiman (1032–?), the Karakhanids attempted to expand their empire and campaigned against the rulers of Khwarezm.

In 1040 Ibrahim bin Nasr (ruled 1040–1068), a member of the royal family, initiated a revolt and declared himself supreme ruler. He moved his royal family into the city of Samarqand, his capital. This action split the empire into two parts, the Eastern and Western Karakhanid empires. Ibrahim bin Nasr attempted to establish full control over the entire Karakhanid empire and launched a series of campaigns in the east. In the 1060s he conquered the Farghona valley, then Chach and Taraz, but Balasagun proved a more difficult target. He captured and lost the city several times. After his death, the Western Karakhanid khanate fell apart and as a consequence, was subdued by the rival Turkic tribal group, the Seljuks (see map 19).

In the 1060s and 1070s the Eastern Karakhanid khanate strengthened its position and recaptured Chach, Taraz, Uzgend and a number of other cities. However, the Eastern Karakhanids failed to bring under control the renegade Western Karakhanid khanate, as the Seljuks provided massive military support to the Western Karakhanid. Muhammad II Arslan Khan (ca. 1102–1132), probably the last great Karakhanid, turned his attention to domestic issues, conducting military and administrative reforms, supporting trade and the arts and funding many public construction works. By 1132 Muhammad Arslan Khan felt he was powerful enough to yet again challenge the Seljuks, but was defeated and killed in a decisive battle at Samarqand.

As with many other nomadic empires, the Karakhanids' end overtook them due to a protracted succession struggle. The weakened Eastern Karakhanids faced a new and powerful rival, the Karakitais (also Kara Kitans), a tribal confederation probably of Mongol origin (Biran 2005), that conquered the territories of Kashgar and Jetysuu in the 1130s. The Eastern Karakhanids were defeated first, below the city of Balasagun in 1134. The Western Karakhanids then attempted to stop the Karakitais, but lost a major battle before the city of Khojand in 1137. The final, decisive battle took place in an area close to Samarqand in 1141. The Karakhanids lost despite help from the Seljuks and were reduced to vassalage in the Karakitai khanate. Members of the Karakhanid family continued to govern small and medium-sized principalities in the territory of Maveranahr and Jetysuu for another 70 years, but in 1211 both the Karakitais and Karakhanids were defeated by the rulers of Khwarezm, and the dynasty came to an end.

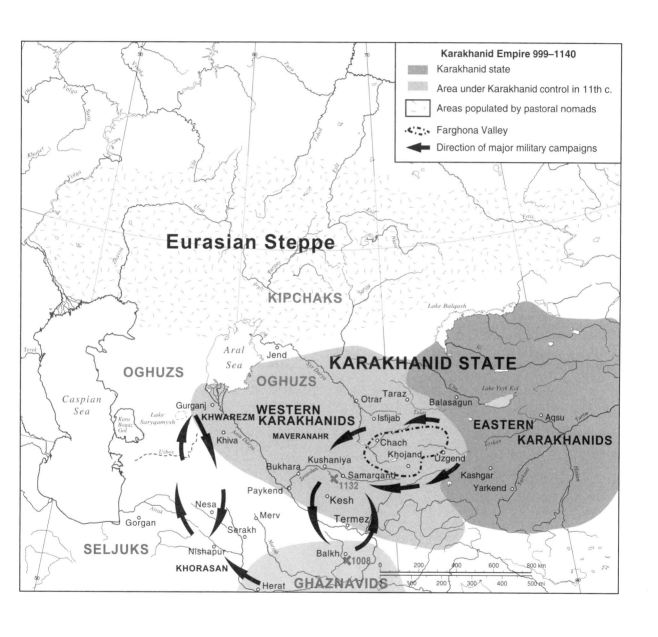

Eurasian Steppe

KIPCHAKS

KARAKHANID STATE

OGHUZS

Aral
Sea

Jend

OGHUZS

**WESTERN
KARAKHANIDS**

MAVERANAHR

**EASTERN
KARAKHANIDS**

Caspian
Sea

Kara
Bogaz
Gol

Lake
Saryqamysh

Gurganj
KHWAREZM

Khiva

Otrar

Taraz

Isfijab

Balasagun

Lake Ysyk Kol

Aqsu

Chach

Khojand

Uzgend

Kashgar

Yarkend

Bukhara

Kushaniya

Paykend

Samarqand
1132

Kesh

Merv

Termez

Nesa

Serakh

Gorgan

Nishapur

KHORASAN

Balkh
1008

Herat

GHAZNAVIDS

SELJUKS

Lake Balqash

| 0 | 200 | 400 | 600 | 800 km |
| 0 | 100 | 200 | 300 | 400 | 500 mi |

Map 19: The Seljuks (ca. 1038–1194)

Political instability within the Samanid, Karakhanid and Khwarezm states, and perpetual military conflicts and internecine skirmishes between generals, tribal chiefs and rebellious members of the royal families, significantly weakened all major players in the region. These developments provided opportunities for many ambitious tribal chiefs to wrest power from other traditional players. Several groups attempted to make use of such moments, but the most successful among them were the Seljuks.

In the ninth and tenth centuries the Seljuk dynasty emerged as a new and powerful actor in Central Asian politics. Seljuk, a local chieftain, broke from the Oghuz tribal confederation and brought his followers to the lower basin of the Syr Darya River. The Seljuks came into contact with the Samanids and soon accepted Islam. Gradually they established control over a vast territory around the Aral Sea. In the mid-tenth century, they moved first to the lower delta of the Amu Darya River and in the early eleventh century to the southwest. Soon after, Toghril Beg (ca. 990–1063) took over the city of Merv, then a strategically important trading center, making it his capital.

Initially Toghril Beg (ruled 1016–1063) experienced mixed fortunes. As an ally of the Western Karakhanids he fought against Mahmud Ghaznavi, the ruler of the Ghaznavid Empire, but he was defeated in 1025. Toghril did not give up but moved to the Khwarezm oases, preparing for a new war. In 1028–1029 his army returned to Khorasan, successfully recaptured Merv and annexed Nishapur. From this base Toghril raided Bukhara and Balkh, and in 1037 he stormed the city of Ghazna, the Ghaznavid capital. In 1037 Toghril Beg was crowned with the title of sultan. This date is traditionally considered the beginning of the Seljuk Empire. From here the Seljuks moved on to establish one of the largest empires of their time, extending their power as far as Central Asia, the Middle East, North Africa and eastern Europe.

In 1040 Sultan Toghril Beg defeated Mas'ud Ghaznavi in the decisive Battle of Dandanqan, forcing Mas'ud to flee to Lahore. In the 1040s Toghril campaigned in various areas of Maveranahr and Khorasan, strengthening his position and securing new vassals and allies. In 1050 he captured the city of Isfahan, whereupon he moved his capital there. From this new base he launched further campaigns to the west, and in 1055 his forces captured Baghdad, the capital of the Islamic caliphate. This action had many important consequences for the Islamic world. It ended the power of the Shi'a Buyids, a strong clan that had exercised significant power in Baghdad and throughout the caliphate. This step decisively strengthened the power of the Sunni school of Islam at the expense of the Shi'a; from this time on the Sunni doctrine became the dominant teaching in the Islamic world. The Seljuks temporarily halted the decline of the caliphate, invigorating it with new energy and leading territorial expansions into western Byzantium and the Mediterranean. They institutionalized Sunni influence by establishing and promoting a large network of Islamic colleges (madrasas) that provided systematic training to Islamic scholars, lawyers and administrators. Significant as these developments were, it was the Seljuks' role in capturing the Holy Land, and their consequent role in the wars with the Crusaders that gave them a prominent position in the annals of history.

The Seljuk sultans Alp Arslan (ruled 1064–1072) and Malik Shah I (1072–1092) took their campaigns ever farther west. The Seljuks conquered Armenia and Georgia in 1064 and crushed the Byzantine army at the Battle of Manzikert in 1071, capturing the Roman Emperor Romanus IV. This battle ultimately weakened the Byzantine Empire and signaled the beginning of its irreversible decline (Gibbon 1788, rep. 2001).

In 1092 Malik Shah I died. The empire was split between his brother and sons, and entered a series of destructive conflicts. In the meantime, Byzantium attempted to utilize the moment and called on Pope Urban II to send a military expedition to reclaim Jerusalem. In 1095 the army of the First Crusade arrived in Asia Minor, defeated the weak defenses they encountered, captured the Holy Land and established the crusader states. Ahmed Sanjar (ruled 1118–1157) attempted to reunite the Seljuks. He moved the capital to Merv and reasserted his authority in Maveranahr in a series of campaigns in the 1130s. Fortune turned its back on Sultan Sanjar in 1141, when he lost his army in a battle with the Karakitais.

This setback notwithstanding, the Seljuks triumphed over the Second Crusade armies in 1148. It was one of their last successes. In 1153 Sultan Sanjar suffered another defeat, this one by a rival clan that captured Sanjar himself and then sacked and looted the major trading centers of Khorasan. Sanjar escaped from captivity in 1156 and returned to his capital, Merv, but he died the following year and the empire began disintegrating. Some Seljuk princes attempted to revive it but met with little success, and in 1194 the great Seljuk Empire finally collapsed. Representatives of the clan survived in Asia Minor and would soon give birth to the Ottoman Empire.

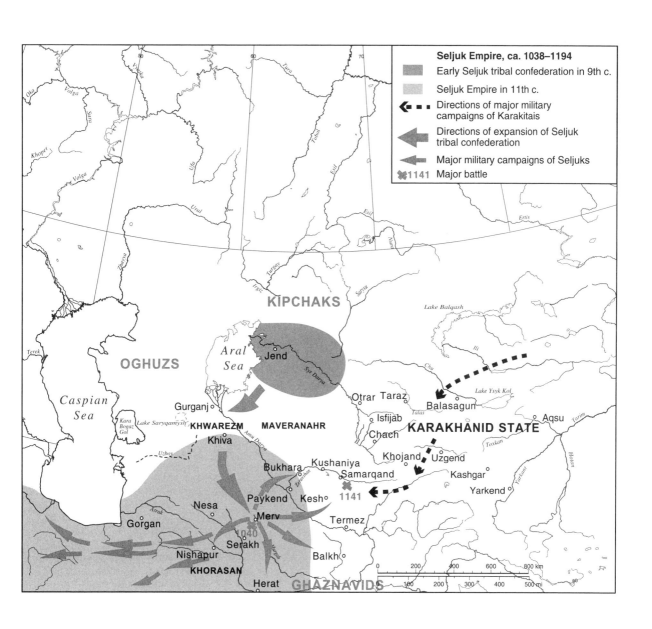

Seljuk Empire, ca. 1038–1194

Early Seljuk tribal confederation in 9th c.

Seljuk Empire in 11th c.

Directions of major military campaigns of Karakitais

Directions of expansion of Seljuk tribal confederation

Major military campaigns of Seljuks

1141 Major battle

KIPCHAKS

Aral Sea

Jend

OGHUZS

Caspian Sea

Lake Balqash

Lake Ysyk Kol

Gurganj

Otrar Taraz

Balasagun

Aqsu

KHWAREZM MAVERANAHR

Isfijab

Chach

KARAKHANID STATE

Khiva

Kushaniya

Khojand Uzgend

Kashgar

Bukhara

Samarqand

Yarkend

Paykend Kesh

1141

Nesa

Merv

Termez

Gorgan

1040

Serakh

Balkh

Nishapur

KHORASAN

Herat

GHAZNAVIDS

0 200 400 600 800 km

100 200 300 400 500 mi

Map 20: The Rise and Collapse of Khwarezm

In the mid-twelfth century the geopolitical situation in Central Asia changed yet again with the deterioration of the Seljuk Empire. In this environment, the rulers of Khwarezm filled the vacuum. Step by step they began gathering together pieces of the fallen empires and building a new empire of their own. As very few players could mount any meaningful resistance, the Khwarezm experienced a spectacular rise, establishing control over a vast territory from the Jetysuu Valley in the east to Merv and Nishapur in the west.

Khwarezm was a small and prosperous principality to the south of the Aral Sea that flourished on the delta of the Amu Darya River. The rulers of Khwarezm customarily acknowledged the suzerainty of their powerful neighbors but retained independence in domestic affairs. The situation changed when Ala Ad-din Atsyz (ruled 1127–1156) attempted to wrest greater independence from the Seljuks. Atsyz rebelled against Sultan Sanjar several times (1138, 1141–1142 and 1147–1148), but achieved only temporary successes and retreated to Khwarezm. However, Atsyz captured the vast area on the lower banks of the Amu Darya River and Saryqamysh Lake. Between 1153 and 1156 Atsyz finally achieved his objectives and moved his armies to Khorasan, but he suddenly died in 1156 while campaigning.

The next ruler of Khwarezm, Il-Arslan (ruled 1156–1172) significantly expanded the state's borders, granting himself the title Khwarezmshah. In his campaigns Il-Arslan showed impressive diplomatic skills, establishing and abandoning many alliances. In 1158, with help from the Turkic tribes of Karluks, he contended successfully for control over Bukhara and Samarqand. In 1167 Khwarezmshah Il-Arslan captured Nishapur and several other cities in Khorasan. These campaigns gave the Khwarezm effective control over both Maveranahr and Khorasan. In 1171 his troops suffered losses in battle with the Karakitais. With the death of Il-Arslan the following year, political power was relatively quickly consolidated in the hands of Ala Ad-din Tekesh (ruled 1172–1200). In 1194 Tekesh defeated Toghril II, one of the last descendants of the Seljuk dynasty, finally ending the Seljuks' attempts to restore their empire.

Tekesh's son Ala Ad-din Muhammad II (ruled 1200–1220) conquered almost all of Khorasan. In 1201 he sacked Herat and Nishapur, and in 1203, Merv. In 1207 he suppressed a rebellion in Bukhara. In 1210, in an important step, his army defeated powerful Karakitais, extending his control to eastern Turkistan and then to the Farghona Valley. In 1215 and 1216, Muhammad II conquered the city of Jend and invaded the territory of the steppe tribes to the north of the Syr Darya River. These decisive victories had a significant psychological effect.

Many small principalities both in Maveranahr and Khorasan and beyond declared themselves vassals of the Khwarezmshah. At the zenith of his power, Muhammad declared himself the second Alexander the Great and moved his capital to Samarqand, then the largest city in the region. He even demanded that the caliph endorse his political supremacy in the Muslim world.

During this period, Khwarezmshah Muhammad II began inflicting increased atrocities on his own people. This alienated many former allies and loyalists. For example, he ordered the destruction of a flourishing oasis around the city of Chach, in order to create a no-go zone for Turkic tribes from the north. His troops behaved so brutally in Samarqand that in 1212 the local population rebelled, killing all Khwarezmians in the city—some 8,000 to 10,000 people. In retaliation, Muhammad II sacked the city and ordered the slaughter of about 10,000 citizens.

Yet, despite these displays of strength, the Khwarezm Empire was beginning to show the first signs of decay. Its downfall was accelerated by a religious rift between the Khwarezmshah and the caliph. In 1217 Muhammad openly proclaimed a move against the existing caliph, and sent his army to capture Baghdad, but Muhammad's troops suffered severe casualties due to unusually cold weather and guerrilla attacks by the local population. Nearly half the army was lost without a single major battle. At around this time, Muhammad made a number of diplomatic blunders in dealing with his neighbors. In 1218 he approved the massacre of an entire Mongol trade caravan and the murder of a Mongol ambassador. The Mongols perceived this as an act of war and moved decisively into Central Asia.

In 1220 Khwarezmshah Muhammad witnessed the arrival of the main Mongol army, numbering between 250,000 and 300,000 (exact numbers are still debated). He decided not to gather his troops into a single army, but rather to spread them among the major urban areas in his kingdom. He judged that the Mongols would have little expertise in storming fortified cities. This proved to be another critical mistake. His troops, scattered among hostile and dissatisfied populations, had little morale for a fight against the Mongols. Meanwhile, the Mongols showed great skill in city sieges: they employed Chinese engineers to plan operations and assemble the necessary equipment for storming city walls, and they used local civilians as human shields for their warriors. Legend states that Muhammad II did not fight even a single battle against the Mongols, escaping instead with a diminished entourage across his empire. He met his death in 1220 on a small island in the Caspian Sea. In 1221 the Khwarezm Empire was destroyed utterly.

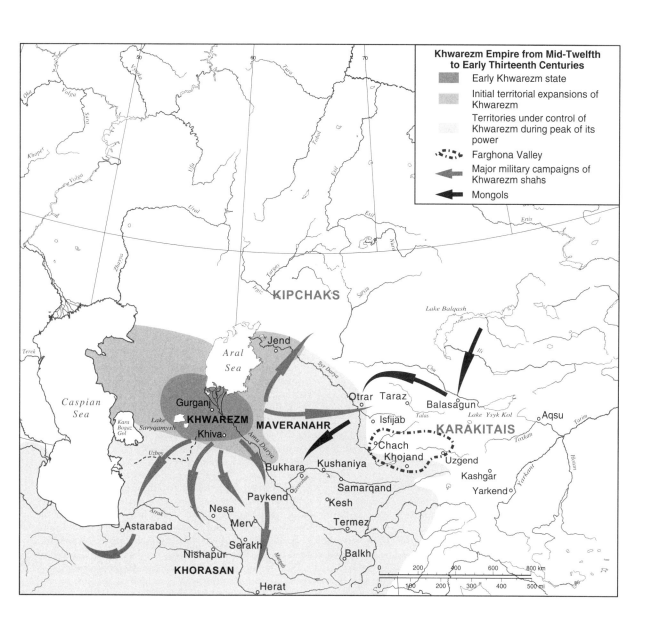

Khwarezm Empire from Mid-Twelfth to Early Thirteenth Centuries

- Early Khwarezm state
- Initial territorial expansions of Khwarezm
- Territories under control of Khwarezm during peak of its power
- Farghona Valley
- Major military campaigns of Khwarezm shahs
- Mongols

Oka

Khoper

Volga

Sura

Volga

Ufa

Ural

Zhoya

Tobol

Tobil

Tura

Esil

Esil

Ertis

Caspian Sea

Terek

Zhoya

Kara Bogaz Gol

Ural

Turgay

Irgiz

Nura

Sarysu

Chu

KIPCHAKS

Lake Balqash

Ili

Aral Sea

Jend

Syr Darya

Otrar Taraz

Isfijab

Talas

Balasagun

Lake Ysyk Kol

Aqsu

Tarim

KARAKITAIS

Gurgan

KHWAREZM

Lake Sarygamysh

Khiva

Uzboy

Anu Darya

MAVERANAHR

Bukhara

Zerafshan

Kushaniya

Samarqand

Kesh

Chach

Khojand

Uzgend

Kashgar

Yarkend

Toxkan

Hotan

Yarkant

Atrak

Nesa

Merv

Paykend

Serakh

Termez

Astarabad

Nishapur

KHORASAN

Murghab

Balkh

Herat

0   200   400   600   800 km

0 100 200 300 400 500 mi

Map 21: International and Major Trade Routes in Central Asia

The establishment of the Turkic empires and later of the Islamic caliphate rejuvenated the Great Silk Road. The Turkic empires controlled the territory between China and Maveranahr and Khorasan from the sixth to mid-seventh centuries, and the Islamic caliphate dominated the land between Maveranahr and the Mediterranean from the mid-seventh to early ninth centuries. Rising living standards among the ruling elite and urban populations generated a growing demand for imported goods and thus boosted both regional and international trade. Craftsmen, farmers and herders became increasingly involved in the commercial production of goods to be sold in the large bazaars in Balasagun, Samarqand, Merv, Herat and Baghdad.

The trade growth was greatly stimulated by the establishment of a stable currency exchange system, and of rudimentary banking and insurance systems. During this era unified legal and taxation systems were also developed. Merchants were obliged to pay a fixed percentage of the total value of their goods and had rights to file complaints (and they did) in the courts or go all the way to the royal dignitaries if they faced unfair treatment. Although there was no change in the transportation modes, and caravans still relied on camels, bulls and horses, the transportation and communication infrastructure was further improved. A far-reaching system of caravanserais was built along the Great Silk Road. As regional and international trade became increasingly profitable, various royal families showed interest in being involved in the business. Historic evidence suggests that royal courts, tribal leaders and the military often had direct or indirect stakes in the international trade. In exchange for various privileges and tax breaks, the merchants and merchant bankers financed the lavish royal lifestyle and funded construction of royal and public sites and even some military campaigns. Many well-established merchant families also carried various diplomatic duties, delivering diplomatic letters, documents and gifts to foreign rulers and conducting surveys of political, economic and military developments in foreign countries.

The variety of the commodities traded also increased significantly. During this era it included traditional items (such as high-quality nephrite jade, precious stones and jewelry, race and cavalry horses), and also silk, textile, porcelain, salt and weapons. Probably, a sizeable volume of slave trade existed due to high demand for experienced domestic workers, concubines and craftsmen in the markets of China, Central Asia and the Middle East. By the eleventh and twelfth centuries eastern European countries, such as the Bulgar Kingdom, Kievan and Novgorod Russia and various Baltic states also joined the international trade, as the Volga River and its tributaries were open for navigation all the way from the Caspian Sea to Bulgar, Tver and other cities. They added new goods to the trade flow, such as fur, leather, fresh-water pearls and honey.

During this era it became possible and still profitable to sell such items as silk and jade to neighboring countries, from which local merchants would carry goods further. This way the merchants avoided the need to travel all the way from China to the Mediterranean and the Middle East. The Great Silk Road was transformed from a transportation highway into a sophisticated network of markets. However, geographical and climatic considerations still imposed significant limitations on the directions of the trade routes.

The traders and explorers used two main options for their travels. One was to go through the passes in the Tian Shan and the Pamirs mountains: Anxi, Khotan, Yarkend, Kashgar, Balkh and Merv, and then to Persia and the Mediterranean. The other was to travel through the broad stretches of grassland to the north of the mountain slopes: Anxi, Turfan, Urumchi, Balasagun, Chach (Tashkent), Samarqand, Bukhara, Merv, and on, once again, to Persia and the Mediterranean. During this era there probably was a rise of the south-north trade, as merchants from Samarqand, Bukhara, Merv, Khiva and Gurganj became increasingly involved in the trade with eastern Europe along the Volga River route in the north and with various states and principalities of the Indian peninsula in the south.

Numerous archeological evidence and chronicles from that era suggest that the trade was quite substantial and the monetarization of the economies of the Central Asian states and empires was quite impressive. The intensive trade went hand-in-hand with major cultural, intellectual and technological exchanges. Numerous educators and scholars traveled along the Great Silk Road opening schools, colleges and educational centers. These centers of learning produced a new class of well-educated local professionals and scholars in Central Asia. Not only did they play key roles in the cultural and intellectual development of their own region, but also of many parts of the Middle East and South Asia. Talented scholars from Central Asia traveled to Herat, Nishapur, Baghdad, Damascus and elsewhere and made considerable contributions in classic literature, mathematics, algebra, astronomy and medicine, among other fields.

Undoubtedly, over the period of about 400 years the Silk Road had its own business cycles, as the trade and cultural exchanges were greatly affected by wars, conflicts, economic mismanagement, currency collapses and other factors. The large-scale trade that had flourished along the Silk Road between the seventh and tenth centuries probably declined in the eleventh and twelfth centuries.

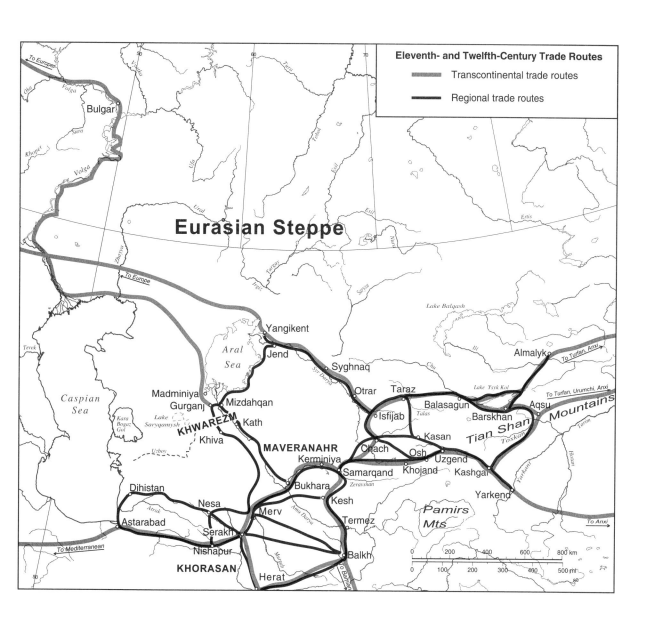

Eleventh- and Twelfth-Century Trade Routes

Transcontinental trade routes

Regional trade routes

IV

The Mongols and the Decline of Central Asia

Map 22: The Mongol Invasion of Central Asia

In the late twelfth century Central Asia entered an era of general political anarchy. Several Turkic dynasties and clans battled each other to establish control over the various parts of Jetysuu, Maveranahr and Khorasan. Almost every leader was forced to fight off claims and counterclaims to the supreme throne from numerous members of his own clan. The general population was deeply frustrated by rulers and governors who wasted resources on never-ending wars, neglecting public projects such as irrigation, policing and infrastructure. The wars became more frequent and more rancorous, as some commanders began randomly executing not only the commanders of competing armies but also entire clans and families. These actions ignited the flames of blood feuds and internecine wars in the region.

In the meantime, in the east a new power began to emerge. The Mongols, a large tribal confederation inhabiting much of Mongolia and southern Siberia, gradually consolidated into a formidable military and political force. Genghis Khan (?–1227), the leader of a minor tribal group, played a significant role in this consolidation. Through a maze of internal wars he rose from the ranks of outlaw and leader of a renegade band to become one of the most powerful leaders among the tribes. In 1206 many of the Mongols were brought together into a nomadic protostate, and an assembly of the tribal leaders (*kurultai*) proclaimed Genghis Khan the supreme khan (ruler).

What distinguished the Mongols under Genghis Khan's leadership from their Turkic predecessors was the use of total war against all opponents. They raised the experience of tribal blood vengeance to an unprecedented mass level. During their numerous campaigns, they did not balk at slaughtering the entire civil populations of rival tribes, cities and towns. Unlike the Turkic tribes, the Mongols were not interested in settling in cities and did not perceive urban centers as potential places to settle or as sources of long-term revenue. In the case of Central Asia, therefore, they stripped cities of their most valuable assets and then often burned those cities to the ground. The Mongols accepted the total submission of other tribal groups and recruited highly qualified local experts, integrating them without hesitation into their multinational armies. For example, they incorporated the most capable Chinese military engineers and weaponry experts into special units commanded by Mongol generals.

Between 1211 and 1219 the Mongols established control over eastern Turkistan. In 1219 Genghis Khan invaded Central Asia and captured all the most important cities in the Jetysuu, including such large urban centers as Otrar, Taraz and Balasagun. In 1220 the invaders moved on the major cities in Maveranahr. The Mongols destroyed Khwarezmshah's army that had been divided into city-garrisons, simply had no fighting morale, and on many occasions had come into conflict with the local populations.

In winter 1220 the Mongols encircled the city of Bukhara, which had some of the most advanced fortifications in the region; the local garrison abandoned the city. The Mongols successfully stormed the defenses, slaughtering nearly half the civilian population and taking the other half as slaves, and then burned the city to the ground. In March, Genghis Khan's army sacked and destroyed Samarqand. Over the summer of that year the Mongols captured most of the cities in the Farghona and Zeravshan valleys, often burning them down. In 1221 they stormed Gurganj, one of Khwarezm's largest and important urban centers. After a prolonged resistance, the city was taken and completely destroyed. The Mongols not only massacred its entire population, they also destroyed a sophisticated network of irrigation dams, creating an environmental catastrophe for the whole area.

In the same year, Genghis Khan crossed the Amu Darya River and within a year or two had captured all the major urban centers of Khorasan. The cities of Merv, Nishapur, Herat, Balkh, Ghazna and Bamian were destroyed with such ferocity that some never recovered. The Mongols marauded at will all the way to the Indus River in the south and to the Euphrates in the southwest.

By 1222 most areas of Jetysuu, Maveranahr and Khorasan had been captured and brought under Mongol control, though the invading troops spent another two years subduing small garrisons in the remote areas of the region, including the Eurasian steppe north of the Aral Sea. Once this subjugation of an entire region had been accomplished, Genghis Khan decided to return to Mongolia, refusing to establish his capital in any of the captured urban centers in Central Asia.

The three years of the main Mongol campaigns in Central Asia brought massive consequences. The region lost a significant proportion of its population, especially educated and skilled professionals. Estimates of human losses vary between two and four million people out of a total population of between 10 and 16 million. The entire economy of the region was destroyed, as well as local, regional and international trade with prosperous neighbors in the south and west. Many cities and areas took from 30 to 50 years to recover; some never recovered at all.

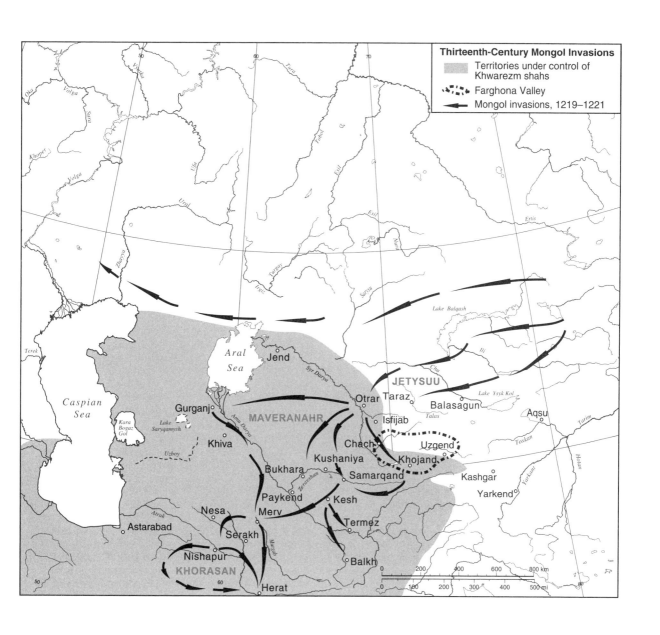

Thirteenth-Century Mongol Invasions

Territories under control of
Khwarezm shahs

Farghona Valley

Mongol invasions, 1219–1221

Map 23: Central Asia under the Mongols

After the death of Genghis Khan in 1227 the Mongol Empire quickly disintegrated. In accordance with nomadic tribal traditions, the empire was divided among members of Genghis Khan's family. In theory, the descendants of Genghis Khan were subordinate to the supreme ruler (Great Khan), who could endorse or take away those principalities (*uluses*) with the approval of the tribal congress (*kurultai*). In reality, however, this arrangement was open to dispute by numerous contenders. Such internal disagreements notwithstanding, in the 1240s and 1260s the Mongols were still able to preserve their unity for major military campaigns in the south, east and west.

The Mongol Empire was initially divided between four Hordes (*Uluses*), each ruled by a khan: the *Ulus* of Tolui Khan, the *Ulus* of Odygei Khan, the *Ulus* of Chagatai Khan and the *Ulus* of Jochi Khan (after his death, Batu Khan).

The *Ulus* of Tolui. Tolui Khan (ruled 1227–1232) inherited the territory of Mongolia proper and presided over the election of the Great Khan, as a regent from 1227–1229. He supported his brother Odygei. After the death of Tolui Khan, the *ulus* was absorbed into the Great *Ulus* of Odygei.

The *Ulus* of Odygei. Odygei Khan (ruled 1229–1241) received the crown of the Great Khan and was recognized as supreme ruler by all Mongol princes. He led the prolonged conquest of China. After his death, his successors struggled to establish their authority and recognition among all members of the royal family and eventually slipped into a long series of internecine conflicts. The situation stabilized, however, under Kublai Khan (ruled 1260–1294). Kublai Khan had successfully fought off all contenders and proceeded with the conquest of China, crushing the Song dynasty. Kublai recognized the importance of China for the future of the Mongol Empire and in 1264 moved his capital to Khanbaliq (present-day Beijing). In 1271 (other sources give 1279) he formally declared the establishment of the Yuan dynasty, which existed for nearly 200 years.

The *Ulus* of Chagatai. Chagatai Khan (1227–1241) received under his rule parts of eastern Turkistan and Maveranahr, and established his capital in the city of Almalyq in eastern Turkistan (formerly Eastern Turkic Khanate). The descendants of Chagatai strengthened their control over Altai, Jetysuu and Maveranahr, and wrested some territories from the other Mongol khans. This dynasty would maintain its control in Transoxiana for nearly 120 years and its princes would play an important role in both eastern and western Turkistan for several centuries.

The *Ulus* of Jochi. Jochi died before Genghis Khan and this *ulus* was given to his son Batu (ruled 1227–1255). The territory of this khanate (symbolically divided into the Blue Horde [eastern part] and White Horde [western part] and later united into the Golden Horde) included all the land west of the Balqash Lake and the Ural Mountains. Under the leadership of Batu Khan the Mongols conquered the Volga Bulgars, the Caucasus and a number of Russian principalities, and raided Poland and Hungary. Batu founded his capital, Sarai, on the lower reaches of the Volga River. The Horde would exist for about 300 years, benefiting from the tributes of vassal principalities and from trade with the Mediterranean, eastern Europe and Central Asia, although periodically it endured protracted succession wars and conflicts.

The *Ulus* of Hulegu. Hulegu Khan (ruled 1255–1265) was sent to conquer territories to the west of the Amu Darya River that were largely controlled by various Muslim dynasties. He led a large army that marched to the city of Baghdad in the fall of 1257. Hulegu demanded that the Baghdad garrison and the caliph surrender; when they refused, he ordered a siege of the city. Baghdad was razed to the ground, bringing to an end the Abbasid caliphate. Hulegu established his control over the territories ruled by the Abbasids and established a new *Ulus*, often called the Il Khanate.

In the 1240s and 1270s Central Asia found itself in the geopolitical center of the powerful Mongol Empire, which at that time spread from Korea and China in the east to Russia and Mesopotamia in the west. However, the political center of gravity moved from the oases of Maveranahr to the Jetysuu area and the vast Eurasian steppe. In 1237 the Mongols left their base on the Eurasian steppe, crossed the Volga River and began their four-year conquest of eastern Europe. About the same time they conquered most of the Iranian plateau. In the 1250s and 1260s the Mongols conquered China and Mesopotamia. Hard on the heels of these triumphs, however, the Mongol princes became engaged in internal quarrels and bloody internecine wars, and the Mongol Empire entered a period of rapid fragmentation.

In the 1260s and 1270s a series of conflicts among various clans of the Mongol elite again redrew the political map of Central Asia. During this period, three important processes began affecting the political situation in the empire. The first was a rapid Turkization of Mongol society. By the end of the thirteenth century the Turks, who had joined the Mongol armies as junior partners under Mongol commanders, began asserting themselves and gained more prominent positions in both the military and government administration. In addition, many members of the ruling elite and with them many ordinary tribesmen began converting to Islam. Finally, a process of economic recovery that started in many parts of the empire in the mid-1200s led to rapid growth in regional, international and transcontinental trade.

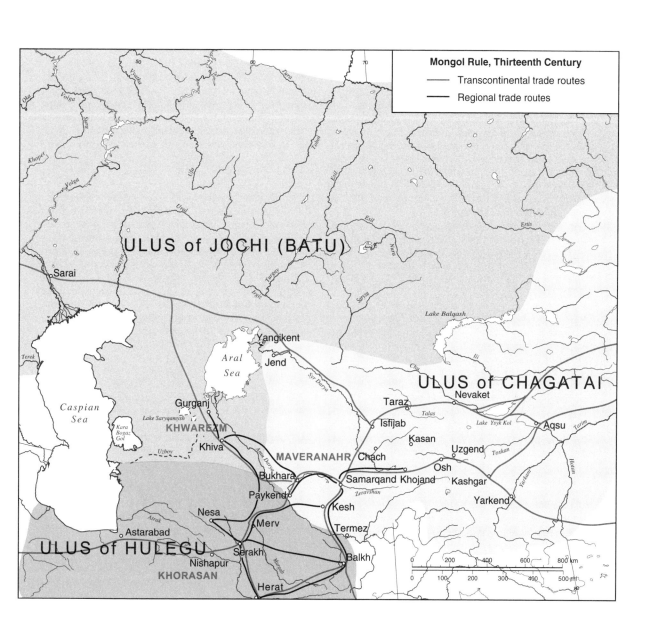

Mongol Rule, Thirteenth Century
Transcontinental trade routes
Regional trade routes

ULUS of JOCHI (BATU)

Sarai

Aral Sea

Yangikent
Jend

Caspian Sea

Gurganj

Lake Saryqamysh

KHWAREZM

Kara Bogaz Gol

Uzboy

Khiva

MAVERANAHR   Chach

Taraz

ULUS of CHAGATAI

Nevaket

Talas

Isfijab

Lake Ysyk Kol

Aqsu

Kasan

Uzgend

Bukhara

Paykend

Samarqand Khojand

Osh

Kashgar

Toxkan

Yarkend

Nesa

Kesh

Merv

Termez

ULUS of HULEGU

Astarabad

Atrak

Serakh

Nishapur

Balkh

KHORASAN

Herat

0   200   400   600   800 km

0   100   200   300   400   500 mi

Map 24: Disintegration of the Mongol Empire

Kublai Khan (ruled 1260–1294) was probably the last, true supreme khan of the Mongol domain. A successful warrior and administrator, he led the Mongols in the conquest of China and effectively administered the empire's military, political and diplomatic affairs. Even with a large pool of local and international advisers at his disposal, however, he could not prevent the process of disintegration of the state. With the conquest of sophisticated settled areas of China, Central Asia and the Middle East came increased involvement in everyday administration and the running of the numerous provinces of the empire. The centralized nature of the state led to lengthy delays in major decision making because transportation and communication technologies were still quite primitive and undeveloped. For example, it could take from six to fifteen weeks for a messenger to carry a letter from Samarqand to Karakorum. Hence many governors and local khans exercised increasing autonomy over various issues, independent of the center.

At the same time, another important factor contributed to the disintegration processes in the Empire—proselytism. The Mongols were noted for their religious tolerance and interest in spirituality. In the case of Central Asia, it is probable that Berke (ruled 1257–1267), grandson of Genghis Khan, had already converted to Islam, and likewise Baraq (ruled 1266–1271), Ghazan Khan (ruled 1295–1305), Uzbek (ruled 1313–1341) and others adopted the Muslim faith. Though Islamization took another 100 to 150 years, the process had a huge impact on relations between the center and periphery, as it created a deep divide between the shamanistic and later Buddhist Mongols and their Muslim kinfolk. Through conversion, the Mongols were transformed from political and cultural outsiders to political and cultural insiders. Increasingly zealous Muslim khans of the Chagatai khanate, the Golden Horde and Il Khanate began distancing themselves from traditional shamanistic practices, thus fostering the political isolation of the center in Karakorum.

In addition, several other factors contributed to the decline of the Mongols' military power, with three probably playing key roles in the process: climate change; disease, especially in the form of outbreaks of a pandemic; and social-demographic factors (a decreasing birth rate and high levels of alcoholism among the Mongol elite). Recent studies indicate that between the late thirteenth and mid-fourteenth centuries, the Eurasian continent experienced a "Little Ice Age." Animal herders were particularly vulnerable to the extreme winters as their animals relied on natural pasture. In such winters the Mongols' horses—a major source of food, their chief form of transportation and the basis for their cavalry—would die en masse, leading to malnutrition, starvation, even famine among the general population. Against this background, the Black Death, the pandemic that killed nearly half of Europe's population in the first half of the fifteenth century, could have similarly affected the Eurasian steppe. Some scholars believe that the Black Death had in fact originated in China and Central Asia and was brought to the Middle East and Europe by the Mongols and their merchants.

Many families in this time were experiencing a chronic social malaise, as never-ending military campaigns took young people away from their families for years, thus contributing to a falling birthrate and erosion of family cohesion. It is not surprising, therefore, that in such a time of social degradation and death many members of the Mongol aristocracy turned to alcohol, literally drinking themselves to death. This might well explain why many Mongol princes died relatively young.

In the late thirteenth and early fourteenth centuries the Mongol rulers were also engaged in a deadly cycle of internecine wars. Even Kublai Khan struggled for recognition among some Mongol tribes; several members of the Genghis family did not acknowledge his authority, including his own younger brother Arikbukha (?–1266). Another significant rival was Kaidu Khan (1230–1301), great-grandson of Genghis Khan. Kaidu Khan, together with Duwa Khan (ruled 1282–1307), a ruler of the *Ulus* of Chagatai, spent almost his entire reign fighting other competitor-princes for superiority in the empire. In 1285, Duwa Khan's troops even took on and defeated the army loyal to Kublai Khan, and began a campaign in eastern Turkistan for three years. In the 1290s Duwa Khan constantly campaigned against his neighbors and rivals in Khorasan, Maveranahr and eastern Turkistan. He also participated in internecine wars among Genghis Khan's descendants from 1300 to 1304 and 1305 to 1306 in Mongolia. He effectively exhausted the Mongol armies in these numerous campaigns, which he pursued almost until his death in 1307 (Biran 1997).

In the early fourteenth century, the conflicts among members of the royal family further sped up the process of disintegration. Kebek Khan (ruled ca. 1318–1326) moved his administrative center from Jetysuu to Maveranahr. After his death the khanate slid into two decades of political chaos and was ruled by various khans whose reigns generally lasted between two and five years. During this era many princes neglected their administrative, diplomatic and political duties and largely returned to a traditional nomadic life, indulging themselves in hunting, small military campaigns and family wars. The political chaos undermined economic development and further weakened the numerous members of the Genghis clan in Central Asia. In this environment, a new regional leader emerged.

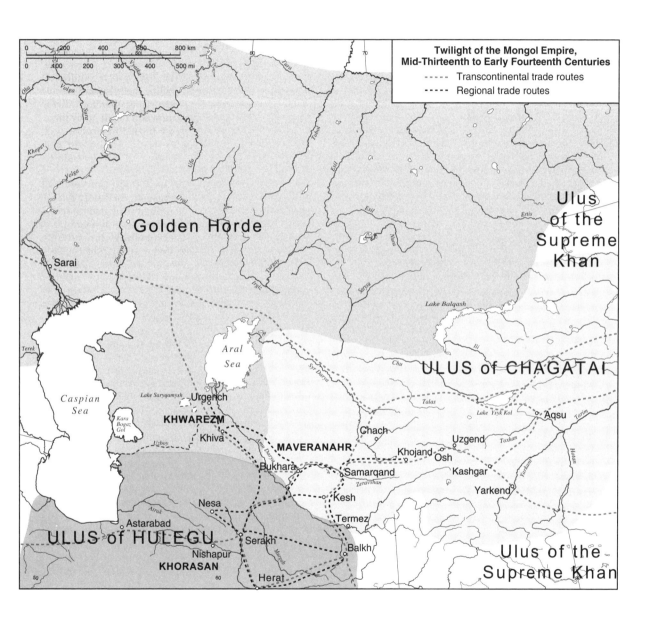

Twilight of the Mongol Empire, Mid-Thirteenth to Early Fourteenth Centuries

- - - - Transcontinental trade routes
- - - - Regional trade routes

0   200   400   600   800 km
0   100   200   300   400   500 mi

Ulus
of the
Supreme
Khan

Golden Horde

Sarai

ULUS of CHAGATAI

Aral
Sea

Caspian
Sea

Lake Balqash

Lake Sarɥqamɥsh

Urgench

KHWAREZM

Khiva

MAVERANAHR

Chach

Uzgend

Osh

Khojand

Lake Ysɥk Kol

Aqsu

Bukhara

Samarqand

Kashgar

Yarkend

Kesh

Termez

Nesa

ULUS of HULEGU

Astarabad

Serakh

Balkh

Nishapur

KHORASAN

Herat

Ulus of the
Supreme Khan

Map 25: Timur (Tamerlane) and the Timurid Empire in Central Asia

The political vacuum created in Central Asia in the early fourteenth century wreaked political chaos throughout the region. Numerous Turkic and Mongol clans were powerful enough to raid each other's territory, to wage campaigns and sometimes even to storm large cities, but they were too disunited and too disorganized to establish stable states or to lay the foundations of economic recovery and growth. In this environment, the major urban centers were interested in investing in and supporting a capable leader who could bring stability into Transoxiana.

Timur bin Taraghay Barlas (ca. 1336–1405), who was better known by his nickname "Tamerlane" (Timur the Lame), was from a small but prominent clan. At the age of 25 Tamerlane formed an armed squadron and joined the military service of Tughluk Timur Khan. Tamerlane participated in various campaigns and gradually rose to high-level officer rank in the khan's army. He acquired so much influence that in 1369 he became the ruler of Samarqand. He found support among individuals from numerous Turkic and Mongol tribes as well as from wealthy merchants and landlords of Samarqand, who underwrote his first military campaigns.

Timur proved to be a capable military leader who enforced iron discipline and instilled excellent military skills in his army (Manz 2002). He employed strategies borrowed from the Mongols, such as totally destroying cities and towns and slaughtering their populations in order to destroy the morale of opponents. He set up special engineering units in his army to assist in the siege of cities. He also regularly captured all the artisans, scholars and craftsmen from occupied cities and sent them back to Samarqand as slaves. In addition, Timur attracted considerable support from numerous tribal leaders by declaring that his ultimate goal was to restore the great Mongol Empire.

During the 1370s and 1380s Timur campaigned in an effort to strengthen the position of his state. Between 1372 and 1379 he invaded Khwarezm, pillaging cities and enslaving most of the craftsmen and artisans. Between 1381 and 1383, he captured Herat. From 1386 to 1387 he conquered northern Persia. In 1386 his army clashed with Tokhtamysh Khan (?–1406), a powerful ruler of the Golden Horde, at the Battle of Derbend. In 1388 he recaptured the city of Gurganj in Khwarezm and destroyed most of it. In 1389 and 1390 he annexed the Farghona Valley and moved into the Jetysuu Valley, colliding with the Chagatai Horde. By the early 1390s Timur, who had assumed the title of Amir (from the Arabic for leader), had gathered considerable strength, establishing a large disciplined army in preparation for campaigning in distant lands.

From 1391 to 1395 Amir Timur's army invaded the territory of the Golden Horde and ultimately defeated Tokhtamysh in a large battle in 1395, paving the way for the rise of Muscovite Russia. The Central Asians destroyed several of the Horde's foremost trading and political centers, including Sarai and Haji-Tarkhan. In 1398 and 1399 Timur invaded northern India, plundering many large urban centers. In this campaign, once again his army used Mongol-style tactics; the onslaught against Delhi was typical in that the city was destroyed, its treasures looted and almost all its inhabitants slaughtered.

Between 1399 and 1404 Amir Timur moved to the west, capturing Baghdad, Damascus and Aleppo. In the decisive battle of Ankara in 1402, he defeated Sultan Bayazid I of the Ottoman Empire. The battle was so fierce that of a 100,000-strong Turkish army just a few thousand survived. Timir reached the Mediterranean coast, but as he had no naval forces and no maritime expertise, he turned back. The Ottoman Turks fled to the Balkans. This military campaign and defeat temporarily weakened the Ottomans and delayed their invasion of Constantinople and southern Europe for several decades. Despite the decisive victory, Amir Timur decided not to invade Europe or Egypt, but to return to his capital, Samarqand.

In 1404 Timur prepared his troops for the last and ultimate challenge in the restoration of the Mongol Empire—the invasion of China. He gathered a great army estimated at 200,000 or 300,000 strong, and at the end of 1404 he moved toward the city of Otrar in the Jetysuu area, as a preparation for war. The winter of 1404–1405 proved to be one of the coldest in the history of the region. Timur, who was accustomed to living year-round in a simple tent, refused to slow down and ordered his troops to move ahead despite terrible blizzards. During this winter he became sick, allegedly catching pneumonia or plague, and died in February 1405.

Timur left behind a large, prosperous, but very unstable empire and a highly controversial legacy. During his reign, he patronized trades and crafts that helped to reintroduce profitable regional, international and transcontinental trade networks along the Great Silk Road. His capital, Samarqand, with its population of 300,000 to 400,000 became one of the largest cities in the world at that time. However, the prosperity of the imperial center was achieved by plundering and destroying hundreds of cities and towns in the conquered territories. His troops enslaved tens of thousands of the most skilled craftsmen, engineers, scholars and artisans, creating a very substantial brain-drain and decades of steep cultural and economic decline on the outskirts of the empire.

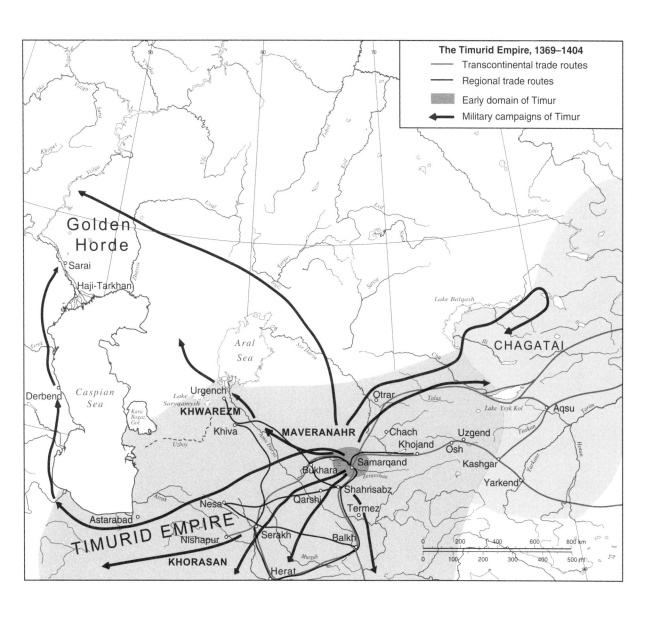

The Timurid Empire, 1369–1404
— Transcontinental trade routes
— Regional trade routes
▨ Early domain of Timur
➤ Military campaigns of Timur

Golden
Horde

Sarai
Haji-Tarkhan

Derbend

Caspian
Sea

Aral
Sea

CHAGATAI

Lake Balqash

Urgench
KHWAREZM
Khiva

Otrar

Talas

Lake Ysyk Kol

Aqsu

MAVERANAHR

Chach
Khojand

Uzgend

Osh

Kashgar

Samarqand

Yarkend

Bukhara

Shahrisabz

Astarabad

Nesa

Qarshi

Termez

TIMURID EMPIRE

Nishapur

Serakh

Balkh

KHORASAN

Herat

0   200   400   600   800 km
0 100 200 300 400 500 mi

Map 26: Disintegration of the Timurid Empire

The sudden death of Timur in 1405 was a serious blow to the unity of the empire. In the east, the rulers of the Moghulistan (which roughly corresponded with Jetysuu and surrounding areas in eastern Turkistan) laid claims on the Kashgar and Farghona valleys and Maveranahr. On the great Eurasian steppe the rulers of the Golden Horde recovered from the defeat inflicted by Timur's armies and began regular raids on the prosperous areas in Khwarezm. In the west, Turkomans regularly raided the western provinces and cities. The greatest challenge, however, was coming from within the empire.

Timur designated his grandson, Pir Muhammad Jahangir, as his successor, a decision challenged by numerous contenders in a devastating series of wars over five years. Only in 1409 did Shah Rukh (1377–1447), the son of Timur, manage to defeat competitors. He reconquered most of the provinces of Timur's empire, establishing the city of Herat as its capital. Sultan Shah Rukh divided his empire into two parts, eastern and western, by establishing dual regency. His son, Ulugh Bek (1394–1449), became governor of Maveranahr, controlling all the land east of the Amu Darya River from his capital in Samarqand.

During the first half of his regency, Ulugh Bek campaigned in the east and north, but he proved notably unsuccessful as both diplomat and military strategist. From 1420 to 1421 he helped Prince Shir Muhammad Chagatayid become ruler of Moghulistan in hopes of gaining a loyal ally and vassal. Shir Muhammad accepted the help and won the throne; but not only did he then refuse to be Ulugh Bek's vassal, he also took over Kashgar and laid claim to the prosperous Farghona Valley. Ulugh Bek organized a military expedition against Shir Muhammad in 1425, but he was forced to turn back without a decisive victory. Ulugh Bek also provided assistance to Prince Baraq to establish control over the Eurasian steppe in 1422 and 1423. Baraq (ruled 1422–1427) won the throne, defeating powerful competitors, but he, too, then refused to be Ulugh Bek's vassal. Baraq Khan severely defeated Ulugh Bek's army in 1427; only the sudden death of Baraq Khan saved the Timurids from a disaster.

These and other missteps in regional affairs forced the Timurids to abandon their ambitions for great territorial gains and to focus on defending the empire's borders and strengthening its economy. During the 1430s and 1440s Shah Rukh and Ulugh Bek systematized administration, patronized the development of trade and industries and supported the arts and sciences. Political and economic stability stimulated the rapid growth of both capitals of the empire—Herat and Samarqand—as well as the other small and medium-sized trade centers on the Great Silk Road.

The death of Shah Rukh in 1447 radically changed the political situation within the empire. Devastating intradynastic wars severely damaged major urban centers of the state. From 1447 to 1448 Ulugh Bek fought a powerful contender, Ala ad-Dawla, who was Shah Rukh's grandson. Ulugh Bek defeated Ala ad-Dawla in the Battle of Herat in 1448. Although Ulugh Bek's troops allegedly pillaged the city, killing thousands of civilians, he was unable to establish full control over the provinces in Khorasan due to the hostility of the local population. In 1449 Ulugh Bek himself was challenged by his son Abd al-Latif (ruled 1449–1450), and lost a battle at Samarqand. Although he agreed to hand over the throne to Abd al-Latif, Ulugh Bek was murdered in October 1449, allegedly at his son's order. Meanwhile, Turkic-Mongol groups of the Eurasian steppe, led by Abu Khayr, had raided the Syr Darya River basin in 1446, and Khwarezm and Maveranahr in 1448. In 1451 an alliance with Abu Khayr at its head even captured Samarqand.

Between 1451 and 1469 Abu Said (1424–1469), one of the Timur's descendants, temporarily restored the Timurid Empire, uniting Maveranahr and then Khorasan. In 1459 he won the Battle of Serakh, defeating a group of Timurid princes and gaining dominance over the principalities in Badakhshan and Bamian (present-day Afghanistan). He campaigned constantly in different parts of the empire, putting down one rebellion after another and fighting various Turkic-Mongol tribal groups. However, in 1469 he was killed by hostile troops while campaigning in the mountains of Azerbaijan. After a short period of further conflict, a kind of status quo was established within the empire as it was divided between descendants of Timur into four autonomous principalities. In the mid-1490s history took another turn when the rulers of Maveranahr and Farghona died, and the region slid into yet another round of internecine conflicts.

The new rulers of the major Central Asian principalities were unable to reverse the trend toward disintegration. Maveranahr and Khorasan ultimately moved apart, their political divide reinforced by a strong religious divide. Shi'a Persians gradually strengthened their influence in Khorasan, weakening and undermining their Sunni competitors. This process gained momentum in the late fifteenth and early sixteenth centuries when a Shi'a dynasty, founded by Ismail Safavi, seized power in Persia. His followers captured most of the areas in Khorasan previously controlled by the Timurids and then zealously enforced Shi'a teachings among the local populations. The emergence of a strong Persian state hostile to the Timurids significantly undermined the Central Asians' position, isolating them from important economic centers in the southwest and from the Mediterranean.

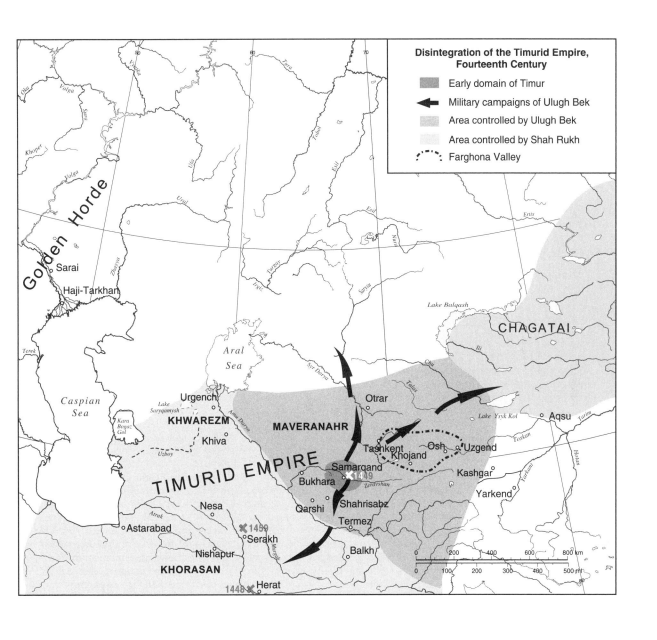

Disintegration of the Timurid Empire, Fourteenth Century

- Early domain of Timur
- ← Military campaigns of Ulugh Bek
- Area controlled by Ulugh Bek
- Area controlled by Shah Rukh
- Farghona Valley

Golden Horde

Sarai

Haji-Tarkhan

Caspian Sea

Kara Bogaz Gol

Aral Sea

Lake Saryqamysh

Urgench

KHWAREZM

Khiva

Uzboy

Astarabad

Nesa

Nishapur

KHORASAN

Serakh

✗ 1459

✗ 1448 Herat

TIMURID EMPIRE

Bukhara

Qarshi

Shahrisabz

Termez

Balkh

Samarqand

✗ 1449

MAVERANAHR

Otrar

Tashkent

Khojand

Osh

Uzgend

Kashgar

Yarkend

Lake Ysyk Kol

Aqsu

CHAGATAI

Lake Balqash

0   200   400   600   800 km

0 100 200 300 400 500 mi

Map 27: The Rise of the Uzbek Khanate

In the sixteenth century the remnants of the Timurid Empire continued to experience a perpetual series of internecine wars. Unlike western Europe where the large cities were effective power bases from which rulers could establish strong absolute monarchies, the Central Asian cities were too weak economically and politically to provide the foundations for centralized states. New khanates did emerge, but they had very short life spans, often disappearing within a decade or two. In this environment it was inevitable that a new tribal leader would gather a large enough army to launch an offensive in Central Asia. Such a move came this time from the Eurasian steppe, under the leadership of the Uzbek tribal elite led by Muhammad Sheybani (ca. 1451–1510).

The Uzbeks had emerged as a large tribal confederation that controlled territory to the east and north of the Aral Sea and had already begun to distinguish themselves as a separate tribal entity in the fourteenth and fifteenth centuries (Allworth 1994). Their leaders traced their ancestors from the clan of Genghis Khan and retained stronger attachments to their Turkic-Mongol roots than did the Timurids. In the late fifteenth century the Uzbeks organized regular incursions into the Timurids' domains. Only in 1499 or 1500 did Sheybani Khan decide it was time to take over the crumbling Timurid Empire.

Sheybani Khan took full advantage of the hostilities among the Timurids and gradually expanded his control from his base in the Syr Darya river basin south into the oases of Maveranahr. Not only did he mobilize a large army between 100,000 and 150,000 strong, but also ordered all Uzbek tribes to move and settle in the newly conquered lands. In 1500 Sheybani Khan captured the cities of Bukhara and Samarqand and established the Sheybani dynasty. He spent about ten years fighting off various challengers, including Babur, a great-grandson of Timur. Sheybani's war against the Timurids proved difficult, as he lost and recaptured Samarqand and Bukhara several times. He captured Balkh in 1506, and Herat in 1507. Though the new empire was established and its rulers liked to compare themselves to the Timurid Empire, its military and political might was not even close to that of Tamerlane, as the state was weakened by economic decline and the hostility of the local populations.

The collapse of the Sheybani dynasty came faster then expected. In 1509 and 1510 Sheybani Khan clashed with an emerging tribal confederation called the Kazakhs (Qazaqs), led by Qasym Khan, and lost a major campaign. He retreated to Samarqand, where he learned of a new threat, this time from powerful Ismail Safavi, Shi'a shah of Persia. Sheybani Khan had little time to recover from his defeat by the Kazakhs and was forced to start a new campaign with significantly weakened forces. In November 1510 the Uzbek army was defeated at the Battle of Merv. Sheybani Khan was killed in the battle, along with his entire entourage. This opened the door for the Persian conquest of major urban centers and oases in Maveranahr, including Bukhara, Samarqand, Qarshi and others. It also looked at that moment as if the Timurids could reestablish their authority in Transoxiana, as Babur allied himself with the Shi'a Persians and returned to Samarqand.

The Uzbeks retreated to their bases in the Syr Darya river basin, but they did not give up. They won time to regroup and defeated the Persians in 1511. A tribal gathering (*kurultai*) elected a new khan—Ubaidullah—in 1512 and the Uzbeks raised a large new army. This reinvigorated Uzbek force marched to Bukhara, where they met the allied forces of Babur and the Persians. At the battle of nearby Ghijduvan the Uzbeks soundly defeated their opponents. The army of Ismail Safavi was forced to retreat beyond the Amu Darya River, while Babur's only choice was to leave Central Asia forever. He moved to India, where he founded a new dynasty known as the Great Moguls.

The victorious Uzbeks divided Transoxiana between the members of the Sheybani Khan family, acknowledging Ubaidullah Khan as first among equals. Militarily, however, they were not so successful in their numerous campaigns in Khorasan in the 1520s and 1530s. But the Uzbek conquest of Maveranahr did lead to a very important change in the region. Most of the Uzbek tribes moved to the area and through interaction with local settled populations began forming a new national identity.

As the Uzbeks were engaged in Khorasan, the Kazakhs, their neighbors in the north, were also engaged in a protracted series of conflicts against another tribal confederation—the Mangits—experiencing mixed fortunes.

In the end, the series of wars in the early sixteenth century, as well as demographic, economic and cultural changes in the region, transformed the geopolitical map of Central Asia. Khorasan eventually came under Persian control, becoming increasingly distinct from the rest of Central Asia in religious, cultural and linguistic terms. At the same time, the Central Asian principalities gravitated toward a common religious background (the Sunni school of Islam), and common legitimacy of their rulers, who customarily traced their roots to the house of Genghis Khan. Poets in the settled areas and bards in the tribal zones began systematizing the traditional epics, folklore and other forms of literature in dialects intelligible to large groups of people. This process in turn facilitated the process of the consolidation of languages identified with specific groups, leading to the formation of new ethnic identities.

Uzbek Khanate, Sixteenth Century

Territory controlled by early Uzbeks

Military campaigns of Uzbeks

Military campaigns of Safavids

KAZAKHS

KAZAKHS

CHAGATAYIDS

UZBEKS

Aral Sea

Lake Balqash

Caspian Sea

Lake Saryqamysh

Kara Bogaz Gol

Syr Darya

Otrar

Talas

Lake Ysyk Kol

Agsu

Urgench

Amu Darya

Khiva

Uzboy

MAVERANAHR

Tashkent

Uzgend

Toxkan

Tarim

Kashgar

Ghijduvan

Bukhara

Samarqand

Zeravshan

Osh

Khojand

Yarkend

TIMURIDS

Nesa

1510

Merv

Qarshi

Shahrisabz

Termez

Balkh

PERSIANS

Astarabad

Atrak

Nishapur

Serakh

Murgab

KHORASAN

Herat

200   400   600   800 km

100   200   300   400   500 mi

Map 28: Bukhara and the Khwarezm Khanates. The Kazakhs and Turkomans

In the early seventeenth century, Central Asia remained politically fragmented while its economy and trade stagnated. This stagnation contributed to Central Asia's growing isolation from the international economy, as lucrative transit trade from China and India to western Europe was increasingly channeled toward safer maritime routes. Central Asia's situation contrasted sharply with the state of development in Europe, where countries were entering an era of rapid economic growth, trade expansion and industrialization. In the area of warfare, European advancements in military technology canceled out the relative advantage traditionally held by Central Asia's mobile light and heavy cavalry.

In the early seventeenth century, four major powers played important roles in the region: the *Bukhara Emirate*, the *Khwarezm (Khiva) Khanates*, *Turkoman* tribes to the east of the Caspian Sea, and the *Kazakh tribal confederation* on the Eurasian steppe. Gradually these powers developed areas of influence. Though there were still numerous small conflicts and wars, none of the main players was able to establish exclusive dominance in the region. The Central Asian states became more focused on domestic and regional affairs; after the 1600s they never again organized any large campaigns.

By 1610 the rulers of the *Bukhara Emirate* had established control of the Maveranahr, Farghona and Balkh areas. They also opted in favor of dual monarchy. Imam Quly Khan (?–1641) ruled the state as supreme khan from the capital, Bukhara, while his brother Nadhr Mohammad Khan (?–1651) ruled from his own capital in Balkh. As in previous eras, the khanate was subdivided into smaller appendages governed by numerous members of the ruling royal family. Throughout the 1620s and 1630s the Bukharians invaded Khorasan on many occasions, but they had little success as the Safavid dynasty of Persia continued to gain considerable strength. Abd al-Aziz Khan, the ruler of Bukhara between 1651 and 1681, and his successor Subhan Quli Khan, who ruled between 1681 and 1702, gave up any ideas of territorial expansion.

In the meantime, the rulers of the *Khwarezm (Khiva) Khanate* were busy stabilizing their own state. For almost a half century, two members of the ruling Arabshahid dynasty—Isfandiyar (ruled ca. 1623–1643) and Abu'l Ghazi Bahadur (ruled 1643–1663)—fought fiercely for the throne. Beginning in 1645 Abu'l Ghazi, and after him his son Anush Khan (ruled 1663–1687), attempted to expand the territories of the khanate to the southwest, colliding with the Turkoman tribes, and to the south, where they encountered the Bukhara khanate. These campaigns did not, however, bring significant gains, merely exhausted the state's financial and military resources, and damaged trade and the economy so badly that Khwarezm army officers rebelled and killed Anush Khan.

Throughout the seventeenth century, the *Kazakhs* were also engaged in a series of destructive wars, fighting for control of the Central Asian steppe. In the south, the Bukharians contended with the Kazakhs for control of Tashkent and the surrounding areas. In the east the Kazakh position was threatened by the Junghars (Oyrats), who established control over parts of the Jetysuu area. In the west, the Kalmyks, a tribal confederation of Mongol origin, consolidated their control over the middle and lower basin of the Yayik (Zhayya) river and campaigned ferociously against both the Kazakhs and Khwarezm. In the north, a new player entered the political scene: Muscovite Russia. The Russian rulers had already captured the Siberian Khanate in the late sixteenth century, and in the seventeenth century they established the first peasant and Cossack colonies and fortresses that would form the border between the Kazakhs and Russia.

During this period the *Turkomans* became increasingly independent players in the politics of Central Asia (Abazov 2005). Numerous Turkoman tribes were spread between Mangyshlak and the Aral Sea in the north and the Kopetdag Mountains in the south, and between the Caspian Sea in the west and the Amu Darya River in the east. They formed an amorphous tribal confederation that was never able to consolidate into a centralized state. Thus different tribes entered the services of various rulers in Khwarezm, or in Persia, or formed alliances with generals from the settled areas in their campaigns against competitors. At various times the Turkomans even captured some districts and cities in Khorasan and Khwarezm, but they usually retreated to their bases.

By and large the situation in the Central Asian region remained fairly chaotic. The khans wasted significant resources in numerous wars in their attempts to grab territory from their rivals. They relied more and more on tribal warlords who were becoming increasingly independent and thereby eroding central authority. As the rulers neglected the economy, agriculture, industries and trade went into decline. In this environment of economic recession, the warring parties were competing for shares of rapidly decreasing economic resources.

Against this background, three great powers emerged on the borders of the Central Asian region and accelerated their colonial expansions in the eighteenth and nineteenth centuries. In the north, Russia was rapidly growing into a major international player. In the south, the British Empire defeated the Mogul Empire in a series of offensive operations and began its colonization of the Hindustan peninsula. In the east, the Chinese Empire wished to secure its western border and to establish control over eastern Turkistan.

Early Seventeenth Century

Territory controlled by Uzbeks (Bukhara Emirate)

Khiva Khanate

Regional trade routes

Kalmyks

Khoper

Volga

Sura

Oka

Volga

Ural

Zhayyk (Yayik)

Uja

Tura

Tobol

Esil

Ertix

Irtis

Turgay

Sarysu

Nura

Kazakhs

Junghars
(Oyrats)

Lake Balgash

*Caspian
Sea*

Terek

*Aral
Sea*

Ili

Chu

Lake Ysyk Kol

Mangyshlak
Peninsula

*Kara
Bogaz
Gol*

*Lake
Saryqamysh*

KHWAREZM

Khiva
Khanate

Uzboy

Syr Darya

Talas

Kyrgyzs

Aqsu

Otrar

Tashkent

Uzgend

Ysskon

Tarim

Turkomans

Khiva

Urgench

Bukhara Emirate

Osh

Kashgar

Zeravshan

Bukhara

Samarqand

Khojand

Yarkend

Yarkum

Hotan

Amu Darya

MAVERANAHR

Nesa

Atrak

Qarshi

Shahrisabz

Kopetdag Mts

Merv

Termez

Astarabad

Serakh

Murgab

Persians

Nishapur

Balkh

KHORASAN

Herat

0   200   400   600   800 km

0   100   200   300   400   500 mi

V
The Era of Colonialism and Nation-State Building

Map 29: Central Asia and the Major Colonial Powers in the Eighteenth Century

The eighteenth-century world underwent vast changes due to the impact of industrialization, a rise in trade and rivalry among the major powers. Large factories and plants in the industrial countries began producing a wide range of products at increasingly competitive prices. Many goods that had traditionally been imported to Europe, such as textiles, began to be machine-produced in Europe, thus undermining small-scale manufacturing in Asia and the Middle East. Many formerly prosperous manufacturing centers across the Chinese, Mogul, Persian and Ottoman empires experienced a deep economic recession. This in turn led to increasing poverty in many of those places.

Although lucrative international trade had long connected many parts of the globe, developed nations' governments now became actively involved in promoting trade, via both peaceful means and force. The British Empire had great financial success trading with China and India, flooding the local markets with cheap industrial products. The development of marine routes steadily reduced the cost of moving goods long distances, making many old land-based trade routes on the Eurasian continent obsolete. Even the largest caravan, fully laden, could not compete in speed, volume or cost-efficiency with a single cargo ship. As a result of these changes, international trade shifted from land routes to marine routes.

The rise of international trade led to rising competition among the major world powers for the new markets.

By the eighteenth century Great Britain had become the leading naval power in the world, capable of sending powerful fleets to major seaports anywhere on Earth. Attracted by the riches of the Hindustan peninsula, the size of the market and the weakness of the local rulers, the British began penetrating India in the early seventeenth century and by 1650 had established about thirty trading posts there. Between 1775 and 1849 British forces essentially completed the colonization of the Indian subcontinent, extending their influence to the north, closer to Central Asia.

Early in the eighteenth century Muscovite Russia emerged from the political chaos and feudal wars of the sixteenth and seventeenth centuries as a powerful centralized state. The Russians cemented their position to the north and west of Central Asia by conquering the Kazan (1552) and Astrakhan (1556) khanates on the Volga River. Some decades later they established a new line of city-fortresses: Uralsk (1620) and Guriev (1645), effectively controlling the Ural (Zhayya) River. Peter the Great (ruled 1682–1725) vigorously promoted international trade and industrialization. Tsar Peter and his successors significantly expanded the Russian Empire to the east and south, driven by the desire to secure the state's southern and southeastern borders, to gain new

land for distribution among the nobility and to access new markets. In this environment the Russians made steady progress toward Central Asia from the north.

The Chinese Empire under the Qing Dynasty (1644–1912) also emerged as a formidable power in its own right. The Chinese "march to the west," as some scholars put it (Perdue 2005), was primarily driven by their need to secure both their northern and western borders from destructive nomadic raids. By the mid-eighteenth century China had established control over vast areas of eastern Turkistan. This action brought the Chinese close to the Central Asian frontiers in the east.

Central Asian relations with the Persian (Iranian) Empire were also uneasy. As the Persian rulers, who actively promoted the Shi'a school of Islam at the expense of the Sunni school, consolidated significant power in their hands and overcame their domestic political crises, they began projects of territorial expansion into areas in Khorasan and present-day Afghanistan, traditionally contested by their Central Asian competitors. The Persian rulers, especially Nadir Shah Afshar (ruled 1732–1747), sponsored an aggressive expansionist policy in the southern parts of Central Asia.

Against this background, the Central Asian states experienced economic and political turmoil, and at certain stages in the eighteenth century they were very close to total political collapse. Numerous tribal leaders, generals and royal clans engaged in endless conflicts with each other. The situation was further complicated by conflicts among five large tribal groups—the Kazakhs, the Kyrgyzs, Uzbeks, Turkomans and Junghars. Political stagnation led to economic collapse on an almost unprecedented scale, probably comparable only with the era of Mongol invasion. For example, some historical chronicles report that the largest city of the region, Samarqand, was partially abandoned by its inhabitants in the eighteenth century.

This desperate situation led to significant changes in Central Asian international relations and diplomacy. Some of the region's rulers and tribal leaders began considering a measure unthinkable in previous eras: turning to the external non-Muslim great powers for protection. By the end of the eighteenth century there were numerous recorded diplomatic missions to the Russian and Chinese empires, in which the Central Asian rulers asked for help with promises of political submission and dependency status. In the eyes of those rulers, most of these acts of supplication carried little weight; they in fact sought no more than military support against competing groups or dynasties and planned to throw away the treaties on their day of victory. But those treaties were emblematic of a new era in Central Asian history—the era of colonization.

Map 30: Russian Colonization of the Kazakh Steppe

By the eighteenth century the Central Asian Steppe was mostly controlled by Kazakh tribes. The Kazakhs were divided into three competing hordes (confederations). The Great Horde (*Ulu Zhuz* in Kazakh) controlled most of the Jetysuu Valley and fiercely competed for control of such cities as Tashkent, Chimkent and Turkistan (Olcott 1995). The Middle Horde (*Orto Zhuz* in Kazakh) controlled the area to the west of the Great Horde from the lower basin of the Syr Darya River and the northern shores of the Aral Sea to the upper basins of the Tobol, Ishym and Irtysh rivers. The Little Horde (*Kichi Zhuz* in Kazakh) controlled the area west from the Aral Sea, all the way to the middle and lower basin of the Ural River.

Though the Kazakhs were a formidable military power, their dominance was undermined by several factors. The settled centers in the north and south acquired new military technology in the form of muskets and cannons, thus canceling out the natural advantage of the pastoral nomads' mobile cavalry forces. The nomads occasionally acquired muskets too; but having no large settled urban centers or technology, they were unable to reproduce either firearms or gunpowder.

This developmental imbalance had very important consequences. The nomadic khanates lost their military superiority over the armies of the settled centers. Hence they lost an important source of revenue and material supplies in the form of the tributes, reparations and military resupply that they had extracted from their settled neighbors for centuries. The neighboring states also began to acquire territories controlled by the nomadic khanates and to redistribute them among their growing peasant populations. With the loss of their military might, the nomadic khanates gradually found themselves saddled with unequal trading terms with their major trading partners—who required them to pay ever-higher prices for various manufactured goods, food and military supplies—while faced with declining demand for their single major export item, horses. Some pastoral nomads began facing environmental problems, too, including pasture overgrazing and desertification and decline in the available pasture due to increasing acquisition of the land by settlers. Studies further suggest that the pastoral nomads also faced serious health problems in the form of epidemics. The diseases in question may have included the Black Death, which supposedly came from Central Asia, India or China, and reached Italy between 1629 and 1631 (the Italian Plague) and Vienna in 1679 (the Great Plague of Vienna). In addition, numerous travelers from the east and the west brought with them new diseases that had in the past been little known among the region's native populations.

Against this backdrop of turmoil, the Junghar Khanate (a tribal confederation of Mongolian origin) launched a series of raids against the Kazakh tribes of the Great Horde. The Junghars had emerged on the northeastern outskirts of Turkistan and had begun moving into Central Asia in the late seventeenth century. They defeated the Kazakhs in a series of bloody battles in 1724 and 1725. In keeping with the era's traditions of tribal war, thousands of men were killed, and the children and women were taken as hostages or enslaved. It was claimed that between 60,000 and 200,000 Kazakhs perished in these conflicts. In 1728 and 1729 all the Kazakh Hordes united and crushed the Junghar army; yet the war dragged on for three more decades. Junghar expansion was stopped only in the mid-eighteenth century, with their loss to the Chinese army between 1756 and 1758. This defeat cost the Junghars dearly. Between 50 and 70 percent of their population perished during the war and the postwar famine, and the Chinese gained control over eastern Turkistan.

Though the Kazakhs proved victorious in the end, they entered the second half of the eighteenth century significantly weakened both militarily and politically, unable to unite their military forces or coordinate their domestic and foreign policies.

In this environment, imperial Russia emerged as one of the most prominent players in the region. After pacifying rebellions in 1676 and 1707 by the Bashkirs (a pastoral nomadic tribal group of the Ural region that had "voluntarily" joined Russia in 1557), the Russians strengthened their position between the upper basins of the Ural and Kama rivers and began systematically populating that area with Russian peasants and Cossacks. The Russian government used the same formula in the areas populated by the Kazakhs: they accepted "voluntary" submission of various tribes into Russian protection, established new military strongholds and began distributing land among peasant families and Cossacks. Very soon Russia established a new line of fortified cities: Omsk (1716), Semipalatinsk (1718), Ust-Kamenogorsk (1720), Koriakovski (later Pavlodar) (1720), Orenburg (1743) and Petropavlovsk (1752).

Noting the moves by the Junghars and the Russians, Ablai Khan (1711–1781), a talented Kazakh leader, attempted to bring together all the Kazakh clans. After his death, however, Kazakh unity quickly deteriorated and a series of conflicts followed. Observing the political turmoil in the region, Russia decided to assert its control directly over the Kazakh tribal confederation. The Russian administration abolished the office of khan in the Middle Horde in 1822 and in the Little Horde in 1824. A small group of the Kazakh tribes were allowed to retain semi-independent and self-governing status under the name of Bukei Horde in 1801, but it too was abolished in 1845.

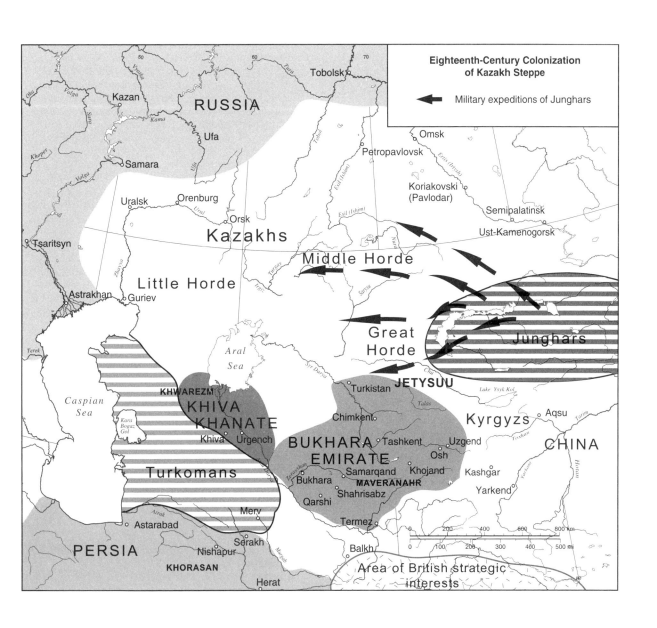

Tobolsk

RUSSIA

Kazan

Ufa

Samara

Omsk

Petropavlovsk

Koriakovski
(Pavlodar)

Semipalatinsk

Uralsk

Orenburg

Orsk

Ust-Kamenogorsk

Tsaritsyn

Kazakhs

Astrakhan

Guriev

Little Horde

Middle Horde

Junghars

Great
Horde

Aral
Sea

Caspian
Sea

JETYSUU

Lake Ysyk Kol

Turkistan

Kyrgyzs

Aqsu

KHWAREZM

Chimkent

Tashkent

Uzgend

CHINA

KHIVA
KHANATE

Khiva

Urgench

BUKHARA
EMIRATE

Osh

Kashgar

Kara
Bogaz
Gol

MAVERANAHR

Samarqand

Khojand

Yarkend

Turkomans

Bukhara

Shahrisabz

Qarshi

Merv

Termez

Astarabad

PERSIA

Nishapur

Serakh

KHORASAN

Balkh

Area of British strategic
interests

Herat

Map 31: Russian Colonization of Central Asia

Numerous internecine conflicts devastated the economies of the Central Asian tribal confederation and of the Bukhara, Khiva and Kokand khanates. In this environment many tribal leaders turned to outside powers for support. In the eighteenth century several Kazakh and Turkoman clans negotiated trade and political treaties with the Russian Empire. In the meantime, some Kyrgyz tribes sent a number of delegations to the British, Chinese and Russian emperors asking for their help or protection. Yet, the Russian and British were initially slow to move into the region.

The situation changed, however, by the mid-nineteenth century. St. Petersburg became increasingly interested in reaching the Central Asian market with their goods, securing land trade routes to Persia and India and halting the British advance toward Central Asia. This British-Russian race for influence in Central Asia became known as the Great Game (Hopkirk 1992). British strategists argued that the Russians might advance to Afghanistan and Persia, thereby threatening British trade and economic interests in the Middle East and in the Indian colonies. Russian strategists in turn saw great economic and military benefits in advancing into Central Asia and protecting Russia's southern flanks from hostile British moves in case Russian-British relations turned sour. The first actions in the Central Asian region were, however, unsuccessful for both Russia and Britain. In 1840 the Russians tried to march from Orenburg to Khiva and lost nearly half their expeditionary army to severe blizzards and abnormally cold winter weather. In 1842 the British lost their entire Kabul garrison who were slaughtered on the outskirts of the city.

Yet, the Russians decided to continue their push into the region. In preparation for this further expansion, they built a new line of fortresses, establishing Akmolinsk, Kokchetav and Karkaralinsk in 1824, and Aralsk, Kazalinsk and Vernyi between 1847 and 1854.

After Russia's defeat in the Crimean War (1853–1856), Tsar Alexander II (ruled 1855–1881) decided to boost morale among the general population by waging a "just" war in Central Asia. To do this, the Russian ministers started a propaganda campaign, emphasizing the need to save Russian subjects from the horrible fate of being sold in large numbers as slaves in the bazaars of Central Asia. In the early nineteenth century, a rumor was spread that between 8,000 and 60,000 slaves of Russian origin were to be found in Central Asia. Relying on massive public support, the Russian Empire made a series of decisive moves into Transoxiana between the mid-1850s and mid-1870s.

Kyrgyz tribes. Between 1855 and 1864 the Kyrgyz tribes in the Lake Ysyk Kol valley, Chatkal River basin and some other areas negotiated a special treaty with the Russian authorities to bring them under Russian protection, a step directly counter to the interests of the Kokand Khanate. This action helped Russia establish control over significant parts of the eastern areas of Central Asia and check any further Chinese move into the region.

Kokand Khanate. Kokand collided with the imperial Russian authorities in the early 1860s. The khan of Kokand was angered by the fact that the Kyrgyzs tribes of the Chui and Ysyk Kol valleys, whom Kokand had subjugated decades earlier, had become subjects of the Russian Empire. Kokand's ruler, Khudoyar Khan, overestimated his military potential and waged a futile war against Russian troops. A small expeditionary Russian army led by Generals Cherniaev, Konstantin von Kaufman and Mikhail Skobelev conquered the cities of Ak-Masjid, Turkistan and Chimkent in 1864, Tashkent in 1865, and Khojand in 1866. The khan of Kokand, having experienced defeat after defeat and mass desertions by his troops, signed a peace treaty in 1869.

Bukhara Emirate. The Emir of Bukhara, Muzzafar Khan, was alarmed by the Russian actions against the Kokand Khanate. He demanded the return of the city of Tashkent to Bukharan authorities and mobilized his troops. In response, the Russian expeditionary army attacked the Bukharan cities of Jizak and Ura Tube in 1866 and of Samarqand in 1868. The Bukharan army, untrained and equipped with outdated cannons and muskets, was defeated. Another Bukharan army, led by Muzzafar Khan himself, lost another battle before the city of Katta Qurgan. Muzzafar Khan signed a peace treaty with the Russian authorities that legitimized the Russian annexation of the territories of the Kokand and brought the Bukhara Khanate under the indirect control of the Russian Empire.

Khiva Khanate. The Khiva Khanate witnessed the fate of the other khanates and did not present any significant resistance. In 1869 Russian troops landed on the eastern shore of the Caspian Sea and organized several expeditions deep into the Karakum Desert, threatening the western frontier of the khanate. In 1873 they marched simultaneously from Orenburg and Tashkent and after short skirmishes captured the city of Khiva. In 1873 Khiva's ruler, Muhammad Rahim Khan, signed a capitulation and peace treaty.

Turkoman tribes. The independent-minded Turkoman tribes resisted and even had some success against Russian regiments below the Geok Tepe fortress in 1879, but the Russian expeditionary army defeated the Turkoman army at the Geok Tepe fortress in 1881. Peaceful treaties between the Russians and Turkomans followed, and the territory controlled by the various Turkoman tribes came under Russian control.

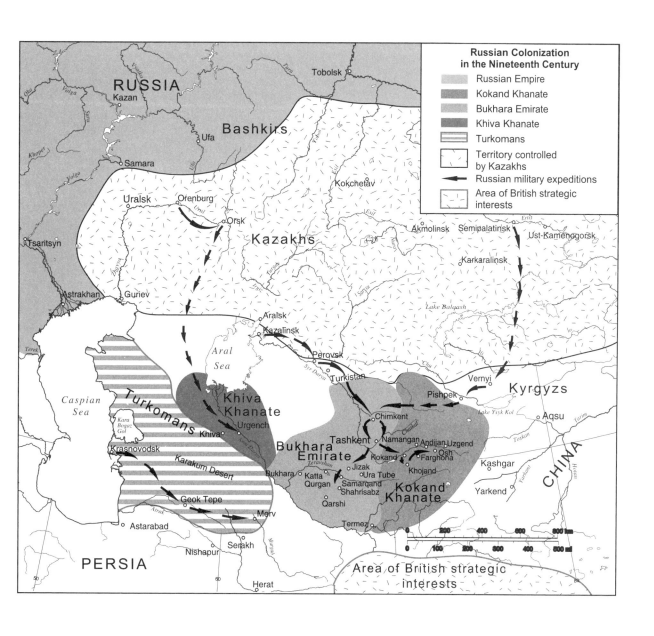

Russian Colonization in the Nineteenth Century

- Russian Empire
- Kokand Khanate
- Bukhara Emirate
- Khiva Khanate
- Turkomans
- Territory controlled by Kazakhs
- Russian military expeditions
- Area of British strategic interests

RUSSIA

Bashkirs

Kazan

Ufa

Samara

Tsaritsyn

Astrakhan

Guriev

Uralsk

Orenburg

Orsk

Kazakhs

Tobolsk

Kokchetav

Akmolinsk

Semipalatinsk

Ust-Kamenogorsk

Karkaralinsk

Caspian Sea

Aral Sea

Aralsk

Kazalinsk

Perovsk

Turkistan

Lake Balqash

Vernyi

Kyrgyzs

Pishpek

Lake Ysyk Kol

Aqsu

Kara Bogaz Gol

Krasnovodsk

Turkomans

Khiva Khanate

Khiva

Urgench

Karakum Desert

Bukhara

Bukhara Emirate

Katta Qurgan

Samarqand

Shahrisabz

Qarshi

Chimkent

Tashkent

Namangan

Kokand

Jizak

Ura Tube

Khojand

Andijan Uzgend

Osh

Farghona

Kashgar

Yarkend

CHINA

Kokand Khanate

Termez

Geok Tepe

Merv

Astarabad

Nishapur

Serakh

PERSIA

Herat

Area of British strategic interests

0   200   400   600   800 km
0   100   200   300   400   500 mi

Map 32: Early Administrative Division of Central Asia

The Russian government faced numerous challenges in Central Asia. In the first place, there was no effective administrative or taxation system in the region. The Central Asian rulers did not consider the Russian move into the region an ultimate defeat, and they explored various opportunities for gaining greater autonomy, including support from the British, Chinese, Turkish and Persian empires. Second, the local population was largely hostile to the newcomers, and tribal and religious leaders constantly stirred anti-Russian attitudes among the ordinary people. Third, the absence of law and order in the region for nearly a century undermined economic and trade opportunities. Fourth, St. Petersburg had a very small army spread over a vast area and was unable to provide security.

The main task of the Russian colonial authorities, therefore, was the establishment of an effective administrative system. Itself a very poor country, Russia operated its empire under serious budgetary constraints. Hence the imperial cabinet opted to establish a flexible administrative system, leaving local governance in the hands of the local authorities and retaining control over major political and economic issues only. Local judges continued practicing Shariah (Islamic law), though slavery was abolished. The ranks of the Central Asian administration were often filled by Russian officers. Traditionally, the highest positions in the region were given to military officials, often Russian generals in the imperial service. All administrative positions at the provincial and district levels traditionally went to civil servants of Russian, German or Polish origin. The whole region was initially divided into several sections, and the city of Tashkent was selected as the regional administrative seat.

Turkistan Governor-Generalship. The Turkistan Governor-Generalship was established in 1867. It included most of the territory that is now Kyrgyzstan, Tajikistan and Uzbekistan (excluding the territories of the Bukhara Emirate and Khiva Khanate). The first governor-general, General Konstantin von Kaufman, supervised the acquisition of new lands, the abolishment of the Kokand Khanate and the administrative delimitation of Turkistan into *oblasts* (provinces).

Kokand Khanate. According to the peace treaty the Kokand Khanate retained its semi-independent status and control over areas of the fertile Farghona Valley. However, numerous riots that were often of an anti-Russian character, and the inability of the last khan of Kokand to stabilize the khanate and establish an effective administration, led to the abolishment of the khanate on 19 February 1876. Its territory was divided between several oblasts of the Turkistan Governor-Generalship.

Bukhara Emirate. The emirate signed a special peace treaty in 1868, maintaining autonomy in internal affairs but surrendering its foreign policy. The Russian Empire provided a special stipend to the emir of Bukhara, and stationed special political advisers to the ruler and his cabinet. The emir granted special privileges to Russian merchants, and Russian officers traveling through Bukhara enjoyed a certain level of immunity; however, the general population was subject to Bukharan, not Russian, law.

Khiva Khanate. The khanate became a protectorate of the Russian Empire in 1873, and like Bukhara, and it preserved internal affairs autonomy while giving up control of its foreign policy. Its khan also received a special stipend from the Russian government and maintained relations with the Russian authorities through specially assigned military officers in Tashkent. The general population was subject to Khivan law, and Russia did not intervene in internal power struggles.

One of the most important achievements of the Russian administration was the construction of a modern communication system in the region. In the early 1800s trading caravans could travel for weeks fighting off marauders and warlords just to reach the bazaars in neighboring cities. This situation radically changed with the completion of the Trans-Caspian railway in 1888 and the Orenburg-Tashkent line in 1905 (see map 33). The railways made trade between Russia and Central Asia easier and faster. Steel, glassware and other industrial goods, as well as grain, were brought to the local markets in exchange for primary products such as cotton, wool, leather and silk. Hundreds of small workshops and plants to process various products for export to Russia were opened in major towns and cities all over the region. New technologies in land cultivation and a better standard of agricultural equipment led to significant increases in productivity. New commercial crops were introduced to local farmers, and many people gradually began to cultivate tobacco and cotton. By 1917 a number of small mines (lead, copper, coal principally) would open.

Such economic and social transformations contributed to changes in relations between the Russian colonial administration and local authorities. As more locals acquired a Russian education and language skills, they were recruited into the administrative structure and army. The new economic realities also began to erode tribal and regional isolation, and to affect the nucleus of traditional Central Asian society—the extended family—as people began to engage in various economic and political activities outside their families and tribes. New types of relations also undermined traditional values and identities among native people, who began exploring their place in the changing world, their relationship with the Russian Empire and the outside world.

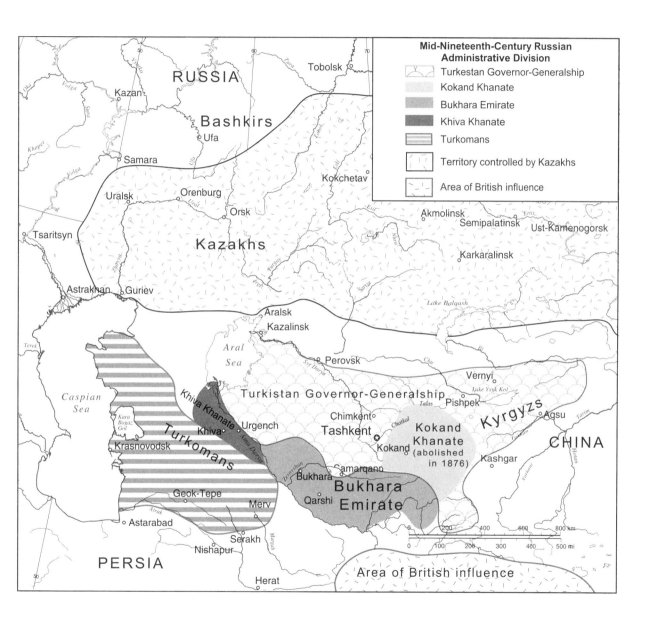

Mid-Nineteenth-Century Russian Administrative Division

Turkestan Governor-Generalship

Kokand Khanate

Bukhara Emirate

Khiva Khanate

Turkomans

Territory controlled by Kazakhs

Area of British influence

RUSSIA

Bashkirs

Tobolsk

Kazan

Ufa

Samara

Uralsk

Orenburg

Orsk

Kokchetav

Tsaritsyn

Kazakhs

Akmolinsk

Semipalatinsk

Ust-Kamenogorsk

Astrakhan

Guriev

Karkaralinsk

Aralsk

Kazalinsk

Aral Sea

Perovsk

Lake Balqash

Caspian Sea

Vernyi

Lake Ysyk Kol

Turkistan Governor-Generalship

Pishpek

Kyrgyzs

Agsu

Khiva Khanate

Urgench

Chimkent

Tashkent

Kokand Khanate (abolished in 1876)

CHINA

Turkomans

Khiva

Kokand

Kashgar

Krasnovodsk

Kara Bogaz Gol

Samarqand

Bukhara

Geok-Tepe

Merv

Qarshi

Bukhara Emirate

Astarabad

Serakh

Nishapur

PERSIA

Herat

Area of British influence

0   100   200   300   400   500 mi

200   400   600   800 km

Map 33: Administrative and Political Changes in the Early Twentieth Century

The Russian government used economic, social, political and even demographic tools to integrate Central Asia into the empire, treating the region as an integral part of the empire. This approach contrasted sharply with that of the British Empire, for instance, which assumed and imposed a separation between the imperial center and its overseas dominions and territories.

Between the 1890s and 1910s, St. Petersburg launched a second round of administrative reforms. The government came up with two special regulations—the Statute for the Administration of the Turkistan Region (1886) and the Statute for the Administration of Akmolinsk, Semipalatinsk, Semirechye, Ural and Turgai oblasts (1891). The administrative structure in Central Asia replicated those in other parts of the empire and was organized at four levels: region (*gubernya*), province (*oblast*), district (*uezd*) and subdistrict (*volost*). The territory of Central Asia was divided between two *gubernyas* (as of 1914): Turkistan and Steppe (Stepnoi). The Turkistan *gubernya* was in turn divided into five oblasts with provincial capitals: Ferghana (capital, Skobelev), Samarqand (Samarqand), Semirechye (Vernyi), Syr Darya (Tashkent) and Zakaspian (Askhabad). The Steppe *gubernya* was divided into two oblasts: Akmolinsk (Omsk) and Semipalatinsk (Semipalatinsk). The Ural (Uralsk) and Turgai (Kustanai) oblasts became separate administrative entities. This administrative division reinforced the division of Central Asia into two parts—Central Asia proper and the Kazakh steppe (Demko 1969).

To support the regular army and police, the Russian government also established paramilitary Cossack administrative entities called Cossack regiments (*Kazachie voisko*). There were four such entities in Central Asia: Orenburg (established in 1748 with its center in the city of Orenburg), Uralsk (1775, center in Uralsk), Sibir (1808, center in Omsk) and Semirechye (1867, center in Vernyi).

Local administration at *volost*, town and village levels was traditionally in the hands of local native leaders. Initially they received their appointments more or less automatically and their tenure was almost indefinite. In the early twentieth century the Russian authorities imposed a requirement that local salaried leaders should receive some level of training and education, and should be elected on a competitive basis.

With the growth of the administrative apparatus, several provincial capitals became dominant in the region. The largest was the city of Tashkent, which became the most important financial, political and military center in Central Asia. The position of the city was strengthened after the completion of the railroad system connecting Tashkent with European Russia (Tashkent-Turkistan-Perovsk [Kyzyl Orda]-Kazalinsk-Aktubinsk-Orenburg-Samara) and with other parts of Central Asia (Tashkent-Samarqand-Qarshi-Merv-Askhabad-Kyzyl Arvat-Krasnovodsk). Various other administrative centers such as Vernyi, Skobelev, Samarqand, and Semipalatinsk also grew rapidly throughout the colonial era, doubling their populations every 15 to 20 years. Tashkent undeniably thrived, its population growing from about 120,000 in 1877 to 156,000 in 1897 and to 271,000 in 1914; Vernyi (Almaty) leapt from 12,000 in 1877 to 23,000 in 1897 and to 43,000 in 1914; likewise, Samarqand went from 30,000 in 1877 to 55,000 in 1897 and to 98,000 in 1914. These administrative centers became magnets for large-scale immigration by both Slavic and non-Slavic peoples.

The rapid development of trade, industries and the monetization of economic dealings brought significant changes to the Central Asian societies. The new economic realities began to erode tribal and regional isolation and traditional values among the people. Families in increasing numbers abandoned subsistence agriculture and husbandry and switched to commercial crop cultivation. Local landlords—*manap*s, *bek*s and *biis*—grew wealthier, while many other social categories lost their traditional tribal and communal support. Some of the poorest members of society left agriculture altogether in search of new sources of income in large urban centers.

Despite all the social and economic changes, however, Turkistan remained one of the most underdeveloped and economically backward parts of the Russian Empire, preserving many of its most anachronistic features and proving unable to adapt itself fully to the changes in the environment. The imperial background to Turkistan's development was hardly inspiring: the early twentieth-century Russian Empire itself remained one of the most underdeveloped empires in the world. The inflexibility, corruption and incompetence of the Russian government and administration in the provinces stirred grievances among social classes across the empire. The first alarms sounded between 1905 and 1907, when various political groups and parties, including the Bolsheviks, organized mass riots.

The Russian tsar responded to these signs of rebellion by introducing the first Russian constitution (the "Fundamental Laws") in April 1906, and the first Russian parliament (the Duma). The Russian constitution stipulated that all citizens of the empire were eligible for representation in the Duma—a contrast with the practice of the British Empire, whose colonial citizens had no capacity to elect representatives in the British parliament. Yet, the Russian legal system introduced a very complex arrangement of representation and elections, dividing the Russian electorate into a number of categories. The Central Asian population (excluding the Khiva and Bukhara khanates) received the right to elect their own representatives to the Duma.

Early Twentieth-Century
Administrative Changes, 1900–1917

|||||||||| Railways

RUSSIA

Tobolsk

Kazan

Ufa

Omsk

Samara

Kustanai

Kokchetav

Akmolinsk oblast

Uralsk

Orenburg

Akmolinsk

Semipalatinsk

Orsk

Ust-Kamenogorsk

Tsaritsyn

Aktubinsk

Turgai oblast

Semipalatinsk
oblast

Ural oblast

Karkaralinsk

Astrakhan

Guriev

Kazalinsk

Lake Balqash

Aral
Sea

Perovsk
(Kyzyl Orda)

Turkistan

Semirechye
oblast

Caspian
Sea

Syr Darya oblast

Chu

Vernyi

CHINA

Kara
Bogaz
Gol

Khiva
Khanate

Chimkent

Pishpek

Lake Ysyk Kol

Aqsu

Khiva

Urgench

Tashkent

Zakaspian oblast

Krasnovodsk

Namangan

Osh

Kokand

Skobelev
(Farghona)

Kashgar

Kyzyl Arvat

Bukhara

Khojand

Samarqand

Ferghana
oblast

Askhabad

Qarshi

Bukhara
Emirate

Astarabad

Merv

Samarqand oblast

Tehran

IRAN

Herat

AFGHANISTAN

0   200   400   600   800 km

0 100 200 300 400 500 mi

Map 34: The Bolshevik Revolution

Relations between the newcomers and the native Central Asian populations were not always smooth, as the economic changes disrupted traditional ways of life and led to increasing social polarization. Local communities blamed the Russians for their growing poverty, loss of land, various social ills and the exploitation of native workers. Anger mounted about the rampant corruption among local administrators. The economic recession of 1900–1903 and Russia's defeat in the Russo-Japanese war in 1904 led to economic difficulties throughout the empire. Many social groups, especially the workers, were dissatisfied with deteriorating living standards and corruption and mistreatment in their workplaces. Various revolutionary groups attempted to channel sporadic strikes and uprisings into an organized revolutionary movement. Between 1905 and 1907 the workers, led by those political groups, organized a number of mass strikes in major cities in Central Asia. Importantly, the newly born Turkistan intelligentsia gradually joined this revolutionary movement. The tsarist administration managed to suppress the first wave of revolutionary uprisings of 1905 through 1907 but was unable to eliminate the revolutionary groups.

A new wave of social disturbances occurred between 1914 and 1916, as Russia's involvement in World War I brought in a new economic depression, high inflation and the burden of new war taxes. This growing dissatisfaction finally gave way to open rebellion in mid-1916, triggered by the tsar's decree to mobilize about 250,000 Turkistanis to carry out war-related duties. Russia's war against Germany was unpopular with the Turkistanis, particularly because it was also a war against Germany's ally Turkey. The Central Asians had a long tradition of close relations with Ottoman Turkey, which was historically and linguistically linked to the Turkic people and had enormous influence as the guardian of holy Islamic places. The 1916 uprising became the most extensive anticolonial unrest in Central Asia, affecting the Turgai, Akmolinsk, Semipalatinsk, Semirechye, Samarqand, Ferghana and the Zakaspian oblasts. The rebels destroyed administrative centers and police barracks, and killed representatives of the local administration and police. It took nearly six months, until late in 1916, for the imperial administration to crush the uprising. The suppression was brutal, involving police, regular army troops and Cossack regiments. Thousands of people were arrested, beaten up or forced from their land and homes. Despite this, some communities and organized revolutionary groups continued their activities well into 1917.

The February Revolution of 1917, resulting in the abdication of Tsar Nicolas II and the establishment of the Russian Republic, did not bring stability, order or any improvement in people's everyday life. The newly established Provisional Republican Government was busy preparing for legitimate elections; it did not end Russia's involvement in the war against Germany, and it conducted only very limited political reforms.

Against this background the Bolsheviks rose to prominence on a promise to end the war and bring radical political and economic changes and justice, including reforms of the Russian colonial administration. In October of 1917 they seized power in the Russian capital, St. Petersburg, abolished the provisional government and declared themselves the only legitimate power in the country.

The Bolsheviks faced opposition from many political groups, the Russian colonial administration and supporters of the provisional government. In addition, the monarchists, who supported the return of Nicolas II to power and the restoration of the monarchy, were prepared to fight the supporters of both the Provisional Republican Government and the Bolsheviks.

In Central Asia the city of Tashkent became a major battleground for various political forces. After the tsar's abdication, the Provisional Republican Government established its authority in the region in April 1917 through a Turkistan Executive Committee. In the summer and fall the Bolsheviks and their supporters swiftly moved to organize elections for the workers' and soldiers' councils (*soviets*) in all major urban centers of the region, with the Tashkent Council acting as Central Council, thereby creating a central Bolshevik authority in the region. However, in most of the small towns and cities on the Kazakh steppe, especially in the areas dominated by the Cossacks, the pro-monarchist forces remained the major power.

Most of the Central Asian elite developed strong hostility toward the "godless" Bolsheviks, but some groups of native intellectuals supported them. The revolutionary groups in the major urban areas organized their followers with great energy, taking over the old administrative structures. Ordinary people, both locals and new settlers, initially remained politically inert, although they were inclined to support their tribal and community leaders. Yet, the revolution deeply polarized the Turkistani population and quickly escalated into civil war and political anarchy. A rifle and revolver became the frequently used method of resolving disagreements, and various political groups began fighting each other and brutalizing civilians in a merciless war.

The revolution also gave great impetus to rising anticolonial, pro-independence sentiment and nationalism in the region. Local intellectuals became heavily involved in region-wide debates about the future of Turkistan and Turkistan society, learning about various ideas, from the nationalism in the Kazakh land to pan-Turkism and pan-Islamism.

Political Development and Bolshevik Revolution

Border of Central Asian region

Railways

Major uprising against tsarist government (1905–1907)

Areas of uprising against tsarist government (1916)

Areas of major uprisings (1916)

Provincial borders

RUSSIA

Tobolsk

Kazan

Ufa

Samara

Uralsk   Orenburg

Tsaritsyn

Aktubinsk

Astrakhan   Guriev

Caspian Sea

Kara Bogaz Gol

Krasnovodsk

Kyzyl Arvat

Askhabad

Astarabad

Tehran

PERSIA

Herat

AFGHANISTAN

Kustanai   Kokchetav

Akmolinsk oblast

Akmolinsk

Semipalatinsk

Ust-Kamenogorsk

Semipalatinsk oblast

Karkaralinsk

Lake Balqash

Orsk

Turgai oblast

Ural oblast

Kazalinsk

Aral Sea

Perovsk (Kyzyl Orda)

Turkistan

Semirechye oblast

Vernyi

Pishpek   *Lake Ysyk Kol*   Aqsu

CHINA

Syr Darya oblast

Chimkent

Khiva Khanate

Urgench

Khiva

Zakaspian oblast

Tashkent

Namangan

Kokand   Osh

Samarqand   Khojand   Kashgar

Bukhara   Qarshi

Bukhara Emirate

Merv

Ferghana oblast

Samarqand oblast

200   400   600   800 km

100   200   300   400   500 mi

Map 35: Creation of the Turkistan Autonomous Soviet Socialist Republic

The political chaos of the two revolutions of 1917 had especially negative effects on the administrative systems in Central Asia. Widely disparate political groups across the whole region, including the emerging nationalist intelligentsia in Central Asia, competed for power in the postimperial era. In this environment of uncertainty, multiple centers of power emerged that often relied on local warlords. The warlords often exploited intertribal grievances, espoused populist policies and were responsible for atrocities against ethnic and religious minorities that ignited the first flames of the disastrous civil war. Many peripheral districts and towns became semi-independent quasi fiefdoms for local rulers, adventurers and even criminals.

The political forces were many and diverse, including supporters of the provisional government, monarchists and local Islamic, nationalist and tribal leaders. As none of the rival groups or parties had the sufficient strength or influence to gain the upper hand over the vast Central Asian region, a number of groups tried to establish their own governance systems. By late 1917 and early 1918, multiple centers of political power had emerged in Central Asia, and several different governments were operating simultaneously. However, they all stopped short of declaring their independence from Russia, unlike Finland, the Baltic states and Azerbaijan. Four of these governments became particularly prominent and left a significant mark on the political development of the region: the nationalist Alash Orda in Kazakh areas; the "autonomous" government in Kokand; the Trans-Caspian government in Askhabad; and the Soviet government in Tashkent.

The *Alash Orda* **government** emerged in December 1917 on the Central Asian steppe and established its "autonomy," with its center at the city of Orenburg. This organization was led by a group of nationalistically inspired Kazakh intelligentsia who won fairly wide support among Kazakhs for their attempts to create a fair and comprehensive system of native representation and establish law and order. It is not clear, and is to this day the subject of academic debate, whether the Alash Orda effectively administered the Kazakh areas and whether it enjoyed the support of the Kazakh population overall, but its autonomy survived for nearly two years until it was crushed in November 1919.

The **Kokand Autonomous Government** emerged in November 1917 as representatives of the native population and Islamic groups gathered in Kokand to establish autonomy. Numerous negotiations on power sharing with the Bolsheviks, monarchists and other groups took place in late 1917 and early 1918, but all failed. This government also failed to establish effective administrative institutions or an army. Despite this ineffectuality, the Soviet authorities in Tashkent perceived the Kokand regime as a threat. The Red Army moved to Kokand and, after a short siege, forced the Kokand Autonomous Government to flee. After its fall, however, the government's many supporters and followers, who were dispersed around the Farghona Valley and surrounding areas, joined a resistance movement called the *basmachi* movement. They waged a guerrilla war against the Red Army and maintained control of a number of cities and towns in the area until 1920.

A group of local activists established a semi-independent **Trans-Caspian Province Government**, with its center in Askhabad. They repelled the Bolsheviks with the support of the British mission in Iran and regular British Army units. Here again, a native-led administration formed an autonomous government and attempted to negotiate power sharing with the Bolsheviks, but failed. Though the government did not put forward any demands for full independence, the Russian authorities saw their stance in extreme terms, and accused the British of harboring plans to split the resources-rich area off from Bolshevik Russia. The Trans-Caspian Government survived until late 1919 and early 1920.

The **Soviet Government** was established in Tashkent in November 1917 by the Russian-dominated Congress of Soviets. The Bolshevik Party in Central Asia emerged as the only politically organized power able to fill the vacuum in October 1917. The Bolsheviks did not hesitate to use the Red Terror against the bourgeoisie, landlords and other exploiters. Initially the Soviet Government was significantly undermined by internal rivalries and weak representation in many areas of the Central Asian region, but it managed to attract growing support by inviting native intelligentsia into the government, and by initiating administrative, political and economic reforms. In a step designed to establish themselves firmly in Central Asia, the Soviet authorities promised to support the nationalist drive and to break with the tsarist practice of suppressing cultural and political developments on the outskirts of the empire. On 30 April 1918, the All-Turkistan Congress of Soviets declared the establishment of the Turkistan Autonomous Soviet Socialist Republic (TASSR), with its center in Tashkent.

During this period the Bukhara Emirate enjoyed almost full independence, but its ruler, Sayyid Alim Khan, chose a cautious path, stopping short of a radical breaking of ties with the authorities in Russia. In the Khiva Khanate, local tribal leaders and generals decided to utilize the momentum they had gained to strive for maximum autonomy, and they forced the Russian troops to withdraw from the area.

Postrevolution Power Centers, 1917–1918

⠿⠿⠿	Railways
	Turkistan ASSR
	Center of Kokand Autonomous Government
	Center of Soviet Government (TASSR)
	Center of Alash Orda Government
	Center of Trans-Caspian Government

RUSSIA

Tobolsk

Kazan

Ufa

Samara

Orenburg

Uralsk

Orsk

Aktubinsk

Kustanai

Kokchetav

Akmolinsk

Semipalatinsk

Ust-Kamenogorsk

Tsaritsyn

Astrakhan

Guriev

Karkaralinsk

Lake Balqash

Kazalinsk

Aral Sea

Perovsk (Kyzyl Orda)

Turkistan

Vernyi

Pishpek

CHINA

Caspian Sea

Khiva Khanate

Kara Bogaz Gol

Chimkent

Lake Ysyk Kol

Aqsu

Krasnovodsk

Urgench

Khiva

Tashkent

Namangan

Osh

Kokand

Kashgar

Kyzyl Arvat

Askhabad

Bukhara

Samarqand

Bukhara Emirate

Qarshi

Merv

Astarabad

Tehran

PERSIA

Herat

AFGHANISTAN

0   200   400   600   800 km
0   100   200   300   400   500 mi

Map 36: Civil War in Central Asia

The Bolshevik Revolution unleashed a multitude of grievances and discords that had been gathering momentum within the Russian Empire for decades: from social and class conflict to nationalism, from interethnic and intertribal melees to deep-seated rural-urban divisions. In addition, the Bolsheviks, who had disbanded the tsarist administration, faced economic and political anarchy and resistance across the country. To control the situation they attempted to use mass Red Terror, similar to the Terror of the French Revolution, against all their opponents, who in retaliation launched anti-Bolshevik terror campaigns themselves.

Between fall 1917 and spring 1918, the Bolsheviks established strongholds in Tashkent and a few urban centers with large army and Russian worker presence, such as Aulie Ata, Pishpek and Samarqand. In many other areas, they faced steep resistance from political groups. The monarchist, Cossack and some national liberation groups challenged the Bolsheviks on the vast Kazakh steppe. Local Islamic and national liberation groups and tribal leaders fought the Bolsheviks to the south of Tashkent. The national liberation groups with the help of British forces repelled the Red Army from the Zakaspian oblast. The Khiva Khanate and Bukhara Emirate tightened political control in their constituencies and expelled all political groups sympathetic to the Bolsheviks.

By mid-1918 the forces hostile to the Bolsheviks controlled between 70 and 80 percent of the Central Asian territory. The escalation of the civil war and the intensity of the fighting meant that neither Bolshevik nor anti-Bolshevik groups showed any mercy to their adversaries, prisoners of war or those in the local population who provided support to rival groups. The pro-tsarist White Army regularly executed members of the Bolshevik Party while Red Army soldiers systematically eliminated their adversaries. As the atrocities of the civil war increased, most people in the region had no choice but to take sides. Native populations often set up their own militias, frequently led by ambitious commanders, tribal leaders or sometimes simply adventurers. These militia groups were known as the *basmachi* (from the Turkic word *basma*, assault). The *basmachi* fought against either the Bolsheviks or the representatives of the White Army or both.

Between mid-1918 and mid-1919 the Red Army in Central Asia was on the defensive and was repelled from most of the disputed territories of the region. Gradually, however, the Bolsheviks and their army reemerged from defeat. Their renewal of strength was not merely military, but grew from a strategy aimed at winning minds and hearts. They promised to end the civil war, to conduct economic and social reforms, including redistribution of land and water, and to provide greater opportunities for the local population. The Bolsheviks did in fact begin to involve the native population in local legislatures (*Sovety*), local district and provincial governments (*Ispolkomy*). They also introduced a nationality program promising greater cultural and political autonomy to the native population. Very small groups representing the native population, especially the intellectuals, lent their support to the Bolsheviks. The ordinary Central Asians, especially the natives, initially remained indecisive about the ideology and motives of the various political forces, though they were inclined to remain loyal to their tribal and community leaders.

In mid-1919 the situation began changing drastically. The Bolshevik government in Moscow defeated major counterrevolutionary forces on several fronts, restored the railroad to Tashkent and sent military reinforcements to Central Asia. The massive influx of regular troops helped the Red Army to gradually regain its control over the region's most important strategic centers in the TASSR. In late 1919 and early 1920 the Bolsheviks also changed the regimes in Khiva and Bukhara. Small revolutionary pro-Bolshevik groups had challenged the rulers of those khanates and organized a series of uprisings. In early 1920 the Red Army intervened in Bukhara against Sayyid Alim Khan, the last ruler of the Bukhara Emirate, and in Khiva against Sayyid Abdulla, the last ruler of the Khiva Khanate. With the direct assistance of Soviet authorities, People's Republics were established in both places.

However, the popular resistance movements, under such leaders as Junaid Khan in the Zakaspian oblast, Madaminbek in the Farghona Valley and Enver Pasha in southern Turkistan, continued their fight through 1921 and 1922. These large forces were eventually defeated and destroyed, though small groups in the remote areas of the region and on the borders with Central Asia were still fighting against the Bolsheviks well into 1924 and 1928.

The civil war in Russia proved to be one of the most devastating conflicts in its history. The country lost between one quarter and one third of its population to the war, local conflicts, famine and starvation. The entire industrial base was almost destroyed and the transportation infrastructure was left in ruins. In the case of Central Asia, the civil war continued for several years longer than in the Russian Federation, and came close to totally destroying the region's economy. Like Russia, Central Asia lost a significant portion of its industrial base, communication infrastructure and qualified labor force due directly to military operations. But in addition, during the turbulent years between 1916 and 1922, the region lost up to one third of its population to famine and starvation, extraneous civil war atrocities and emigration.

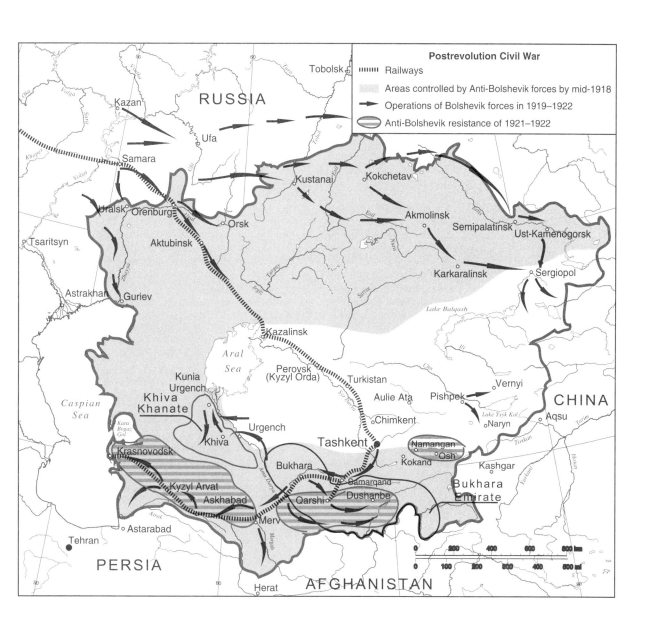

Postrevolution Civil War

||||||| Railways

Areas controlled by Anti-Bolshevik forces by mid-1918

➤ Operations of Bolshevik forces in 1919–1922

Anti-Bolshevik resistance of 1921–1922

Tobolsk

RUSSIA

Kazan

Ufa

Samara

Uralsk

Orenburg

Orsk

Aktubinsk

Tsaritsyn

Astrakhan

Guriev

Kustanai

Kokchetav

Akmolinsk

Semipalatinsk

Ust-Kamenogorsk

Karkaralinsk

Sergiopol

Lake Balqash

Kazalinsk

Aral Sea

Perovsk (Kyzyl Orda)

Turkistan

Aulie Ata

Vernyi

Pishpek

CHINA

Caspian Sea

Kunia Urgench

Khiva Khanate

Khiva

Urgench

Tashkent

Chimkent

Lake Ysyk Kol

Naryn

Aqsu

Kara Bogaz Gol

Krasnovodsk

Bukhara

Namangan

Osh

Kokand

Kashgar

Kyzyl Arvat

Askhabad

Qarshi

Samarqand

Dushanbe

Bukhara Emirate

Merv

Astarabad

Tehran

PERSIA

AFGHANISTAN

Herat

0   200   400   600   800 km

0   100   200   300   400   500 mi

Map 37: Nation-State Delimitation in Central Asia, 1924–1926

Between 1920 and 1924 the Soviet government instituted a series of political changes that culminated in the creation of the Central Asian republics. This very complex process was affected by a number of factors and considerations, and it created outcomes that continue to influence relations between the republics well into the twenty-first century.

The nation-state delimitation started in Central Asia against the background of the devastating civil war. The Soviet concept of "national self-determination" was anchored in the Bolshevik Party manifesto, which promised to break with the tsarist policy of discrimination against ethnic minorities. The rise of national identities and national liberation movements in the Russian Empire was one of the important driving forces stirring mass political participation.

Between 1916 and 1920 a growing number of native Central Asians became involved in the political process and governance for the first time. The rapidly burgeoning native intelligentsia eagerly embraced new ideas ranging from nationalism to liberalism and from pan-Turkism to communism. In response to the rising cultural and national identity, the Soviet authorities began discussing various models for implementing their nationality policy. Three major scenarios were floated in the early 1920s: (1) to keep Central Asia as parts of the Soviet state on the same principle that applied during the Russian imperial era; (2) to create a single autonomous administrative entity—a superprovince or federal republic; (3) to create politically and culturally autonomous entities—nation-states—as part of the Soviet state.

All these paradigms were vigorously debated between 1920 and 1924 by the Kremlin leaders and the Central Asian intelligentsia. In the end, Moscow embraced the ideas of those Central Asian leaders who suggested dividing the region along vague ethnic lines. The Soviet government had already set a precedent with an experiment delimiting the borders of the Kazakh Autonomous Republic within the Russian Federation in 1920 (until 1926 Kazakhs were called "Kyrgyzs" or "Kaisak-Kyrgyzs" and Kyrgyzs were called "Kara-Kyrgyzs"), and the Turkmen Autonomous Oblast in 1921. In 1924 the Kremlin finalized its new nationality scheme and proceeded with the creation of nation-states within the Soviet Union having three different levels of political and cultural autonomy: (1) the Soviet nation-state with its own government and in "voluntary" union with the other Soviet republics (this applied to Uzbekistan); (2) autonomous republic status within the Russian Federation (the case with the Kyrgyz [Kazakh]) Autonomous Republic); (3) autonomous oblast status within the Russian Federation (the case with the Kara-Kyrgyz Autonomous Oblast).

On 27 October 1924 the Turkistan Soviet Socialist Republic (TSSR) was abolished to give way to the newly designated nation-states. Two nation-states and four autonomous entities were immediately established in Central Asia.

The **Turkmen Soviet Socialist Republic** was upgraded from the Turkmen Autonomous Oblast into a union republic with the city of Askhabad as its capital.

The **Kara-Kyrgyz (later Kyrgyz) Autonomous Oblast** was established within the Russian Federation with its capital in Pishpek. The *oblast* received under its jurisdiction significant portions of the Semirechye, Syr Darya and Farghona districts and a small section of the Samarqand oblast.

The **Uzbek Soviet Socialist Republic** was established as a union republic with its capital in Samarqand, and also including the Tajik region as an autonomous republic. It acquired most of the former territory of the Bukhara Emirate and Turkistan province.

The **Tajik Autonomous Soviet Socialist Republic** was created in 1924 as an autonomous republic within the Uzbek SSR, with its capital in Dushanbe. It included the eastern and southeastern parts of the Bukhara People's Republic (formerly the Bukhara Emirate).

The **Kirgiz (later Kazakh) Autonomous Soviet Socialist Republic** was already established within the Russian Federation, with its capital in Orenburg, but the year 1924 brought several important changes, as the capital was moved to the city of Kyzyl Orda. The republic received under its jurisdiction most of the Kazakh steppe, which had been controlled by Kazakh Hordes in the late eighteenth century.

The **Karakalpak Autonomous Oblast** was established within the Kazakh ASSR in February 1925, with its capital in Nukus.

Between 1924 and 1926 the Soviet authorities completed this politically controversial border delimitation scheme, which at the time was hotly debated and contested. Recent studies suggest that the process resulted from vigorous debate both among and between the native Central Asian leaders and the policy makers in Moscow. The territorial delimitation was very difficult in places with traditionally mixed populations, such as the Farghona and Semirechye valleys; the Soviet authorities employed a very complex formula in assessing tsarist-era censuses, population sizes and even community and tribal structures. They managed to convince skeptics that the borders would play purely symbolic roles due to the political and social integration and intraregional cooperation prevailing within the Soviet Union.

Nation-States, 1924–1926

	Railways
——	Borders of Soviet Republics
- - -	Borders of Autonomous Republics/Oblasts

RUSSIAN SOVIET FEDERATED SOCIALIST REPUBLIC

Oka
Volga
Sura
Kazan
Ufa
Ufa
Samara
Khoper
Volga
Kustanai
Kokchetav
Pavlodar
Uralsk
Orenburg (capital 1920–24)
Ural
Orsk
Akmolinsk
Semipalatinsk
Ertis
Ust-Kamenogorsk
Stalingrad
Aktubinsk
Esil
Zhayyq
Irtgiz
Turgai
Nura
Kirgiz ASSR
Karkaralinsk
Sergiopol
Astrakhan
Guriev
Sarysu
Terek

Kazalinsk
Aral Sea
Syr Darya
Lake Balqash
Kyzyl Orda
Turkistan
Chu
Vernyi
Kunia Urgench
Karakalpak AO
Aulie Ata
Pishpek
Lake Ysyk Köl
CHINA
Nukus
Urgench
Chimkent
Kara-Kyrgyz AO
Aqsu
Caspian Sea
Kara Bogaz Gol
Khiva
Tashkent
Namangan
Toxkan
Kashgar
Krasnovodsk
Turkmen SSR
Uzbek SSR
Kokand
Osh
Yarkant
Hotan
Tarim
Kyzyl Arvat
Samarqand
Bukhara
Dushanbe
Tajik ASSR
Ashkhabad
Qarshi
Atrak
Merv
Amu Darya
Murgab
Astarabad
Tehran

PERSIA

Herat

AFGHANISTAN

0   200   400   600   800 km
0   100   200   300   400   500 mi

Map 38: Administrative and Political Changes in Central Asia, 1926–1936

Over the decade from 1926 to 1936 the Soviet government introduced a new round of changes to consolidate political power and newly born national identities. First, all political parties other than the Bolshevik Party—subsequently renamed the Communist Party (CP)—were banned. From the late 1920s onward the Soviet authorities prohibited tribal leaders and former tsarist officers from holding any position in the national government or in the Communist Party, though the Kremlin incorporated many representatives of the native intelligentsia into the administration and governments within each newly created national republic. Second, all political and intellectual debate was banned within the ruling party, especially on the issues of nationality and nation-state delimitation. Third, the Soviet central government introduced completely new political and administrative systems that revolved around the ruling party. Fourth, the Bolshevik (Communist) Party as the ruling party was put in control of all branches of power, administration and governance.

Between 1926 and 1936 the Soviet government revised some aspects of the nation-state delimitation and introduced changes into the administrative and political map of the region. These changes effectively finalized all territorial claims and disputes by adjusting borders and administrative divisions within the region and within each republic. These adjustments also paved the way for the formation of federal relations with the Kremlin.

The **Kazakh Autonomous Soviet Socialist Republic** underwent significant changes, gaining the Syr Darya and Jetysuu (formerly Semirechye) provinces in 1925. However, Orenburg and surrounding areas were transferred to the jurisdiction of the Russian Federation. The capital of Kazakhstan, which had moved from Orenburg to the city of Kyzyl Orda in 1924 was again moved, to Alma-Ata (present-day Almaty), in 1929. In 1930, the Karakalpak Autonomous Oblast was transferred from the jurisdiction of Kazakhstan to the Russian Federation. In 1936 the Kazakh ASSR received the status of union republic and was renamed Kazakh Soviet Socialist Republic (Kazakh SSR), thus gaining the legal right to leave the USSR.

The **Kyrgyz Autonomous Oblast** (renamed from the "Kara-Kyrgyz" to "Kyrgyz" in 1925) gained the status of Autonomous Republic of the Russian Federation in 1926. In 1936 the Kyrgyz ASSR received the status of union republic and was renamed Kyrgyz Soviet Socialist Republic (Kyrgyz SSR).

The **Tajik Autonomous Soviet Socialist Republic**. In 1929 the Tajik ASSR gained the status of union republic within the USSR. At the same time, the territory of the Khojand region was transferred from the Uzbek SSR to the Tajik SSR. The Soviet Constitution of 1936 reconfirmed the status of the Tajik SSR as a union republic.

The **Turkmen Soviet Socialist Republic** was established as a union republic in 1924. The republic did not experience significant territorial changes and its status was reconfirmed by the Soviet Constitution of 1936.

The **Uzbek Soviet Socialist Republic**, was established as a union republic in 1924, including Tajikistan as an autonomous republic. In 1929 Uzbek SSR lost Tajik ASSR, which gained the status of union republic, and transferred the territory of the Khojand region to the new Tajik SSR. However, in 1936 the Uzbek SSR added the Karakalpak ASSR to its jurisdiction.

The **Karakalpak Autonomous Oblast** was transferred from the jurisdiction of the Kazakh ASSR to the Russian Federation in 1930, and in 1932 gained the status of an autonomous republic. In 1936 the Karakalpak ASSR was transferred to the jurisdiction of the Uzbek SSR.

The Soviet Constitution of 1936 endorsed all the administrative and political changes of the previous two decades. It also sanctioned the elevation of the political status of the three Central Asian autonomous republics to that of union republic. The administrative structure in the Central Asian republics replicated those in other parts of the Soviet Union and was organized at three levels: province (*oblast*), district (*raion*) and city (town or village). In addition, the Uzbek SSR had under its jurisdiction an autonomous republic (the Karakalpak ASSR), and Tajik SSR had under its jurisdiction an autonomous *oblast* (Gorno Badakhshan Oblast). Although these divisions were established primarily for administrative and planning purposes, they reflected both the peculiarities of the region's economic geography and, in some degree, the tribal divisions of the Central Asian societies.

Every republic established its own constitution, and administrative changes within the individual republics (such as abolishing and establishing *oblasts* or districts, or changing the status of individual towns and villages) were within the jurisdiction of the union republics.

One of the most important areas of change during the Soviet era was in the cultural landscape of the region. Many old cities were renamed according to the Soviet rulers' tastes, and many newly founded cities and towns were named after various Soviet and Russian historical leaders. The city of Pishpek (the capital of the Kyrgyz SSR), for example, was renamed Frunze after the Red Army general and civil war hero Michael Frunze; the city of Khojand and the Khojand oblast were renamed the city of Leninabad and Leninabad oblast; Dushanbe (the capital of Tajikistan) was renamed Stalinabad, and so on. The names of many small towns, villages and streets were Russified and named after various Soviet heroes and leaders.

Political Map, 1926–1936

▓▓▓▓ Railways

----- Borders of Karakalpak ASSR
(within Uzbek SSR from 1936)

RUSSIAN SOVIET FEDERATED
SOCIALIST REPUBLIC

Oka

Volga

Kazan

Sura

Ufa

Vyatka

Tura

Tobol

Petropavlovsk

Kokchetav

Pavlodar

Samara
(Kuibyshev
1935–1991)

Kustanai

Khoper

Ufa

Orenburg

Uralsk

Orsk

Ural

Akmolinsk

Esil

Semipalatinsk

Ust-Kamenogorsk

Ertis

Stalingrad

Zhaiyq

Aktubinsk

Turgai

Tobol

Nura

Sarysu

Karkaralinsk

Sergiopol

Astrakhan

Guriev

Terek

Kazalinsk

Aral
Sea

Kazakh ASSR
(Kazakh SSR from 1936)

Lake Balqash

Ili

Caspian
Sea

Kyzyl Orda
(capital 1924–29)

Syr Darya

Turkistan

Chu

Frunze

Alma Ata
(capital from 1929)

CHINA

Kara
Bogaz
Gol

Kunia
Urgench

Karakalpak
ASSR

Nukus

Uzbek
SSR

Khiva

Urgench

Aulie Ata

Chimkent

Kyrgyz ASSR
(Kyrgyz SSR from 1936)

Lake Ysyk Kol

Aqsu

Tarim

Krasnovodsk

Tashkent
(capital from 1930)

Khojand

Osh

Kashgar

Toxkan

Turkmen SSR

Bukhara

Samarqand
(capital to 1930)

Stalinabad

Toxkan

Kyzyl Arvat

Atrak

Ashkhabad

Qarshi

Amu Darya

Tajik SSR
(from 1929)

0   200   400   600   800 km

0 100 200   300   400   500 mi

Tehran

Astarabad

Merv

Murgab

IRAN

Herat

AFGHANISTAN

Map 39: Economic Changes in Central Asia

The Soviet leaders believed that only when nations were united by common economic interests could they overcome their "backwardness." Thus, the Soviet government channeled sizable investments into the region in an attempt to build modern diversified economies. In order to accelerate their regional economic growth and make effective use of these investments, the Soviet government introduced five-year planning. These plans emphasized high-priority investments in building major industrial enterprises, especially heavy, large machinery and light manufacturing, and large-scale state-controlled farming.

Kazakhstan. During the Soviet era the Kazakhstani government, with help from the Soviet central budget, built a diversified economy with a strong industrial, agricultural and resources-extraction base. In the 1930s all private farmers, herders and peasants were brought into the Soviet-style cooperatives (*kolkhozes*). It was, however, only in the 1950s and 1960s that the large areas of so-called virgin land (*tselina*) were brought under cultivation with a huge inflow of investment and immigrants from all over the Soviet Union. This made Kazakhstan the grain basket of the USSR, as it provided about one quarter of the total cereal production in the Soviet Union. Between the 1950s and 1980s Kazakhstan also came to specialize in nonferrous (lead, copper and nickel) and ferrous (iron ore) metal and coal production. With the discovery of large oil and gas reserves in the country's western and southern provinces, from the 1970s onward the republic became one of the fastest-growing oil and gas producers among the socialist countries. Kazakhstan also built heavy machinery and aerospace service enterprises. In fact, nearly 80 percent of all Soviet space rockets were launched from the republic's territory.

Kyrgyzstan. Remoteness from major markets, a mountainous landscape and a small population made Kyrgyzstan's economic development especially difficult. During the Soviet era the Kyrgyzstan government made an effort to create its own industrial, agricultural and resources-extraction base. In the 1930s herders and private farmers were brought into the *kolkhozes* and the country became an important producer of various agricultural products, such as tobacco, wool, leather, sugar, vegetables and cotton. Between the 1940s and 1990s about 500 state-controlled enterprises were established, specializing in the production of nonferrous metals (antimony, uranium ore and mercury) and small amounts of coal. The republic became the fifth largest hydroelectric power producer in the USSR.

Tajikistan. During the Soviet era the government of Tajikistan established a diversified industrial, agricultural and resources-extraction base. In the 1930s and 1940s the *kolkhozes* became an important producer of such agricultural products as cotton (third largest in the USSR), silk, berries and grapes. State-controlled enterprises, established mainly between the 1940s and 1990s, began producing nonferrous materials (aluminum, bismuth ore, silver, gold and molybdenum) and small amounts of gas and coal. In the 1970s and 1980s the republic was one of the largest producers of hydroelectric power in Central Asia. In the 1970s and 1980s Tajikistan also began to export silk, textiles and apparel.

Turkmenistan. Turkmenistan developed its own industrial, agricultural and resources-extraction base. In the 1930s the *kolkhozes* began large-scale production of various agricultural products, such as cotton (the second-largest crop in the USSR), wool, sheepskin (the second largest producer of karakul, the famous Astrakhan fur) and small quantities of raw silk. Between the 1940s and 1990s hundreds of state-controlled enterprises were established that specialized in production of the nonferrous materials (sodium sulfate, bromine, sulfur and small amounts of magnesium sulfate). In the 1970s the republic became an important producer of carpets and carpet products (second largest in the USSR), textiles, leather materials and apparel. In addition, from the 1970s on the republic became the USSR's second largest producer of gas and its fifth largest producer of petroleum.

Uzbekistan. The country established a diversified industrial, agricultural and resources-extraction base. In the 1930s the country became the largest producer of cotton, raw silk, berries and vegetable oil in the USSR. State-controlled enterprises specialized in producing nonferrous metals (the second largest producer of gold in the USSR), gas and coal. In the 1970s the republic became one of the largest producers of cotton and silk fabric in Central Asia. In the 1970s and 1980s it began large-scale exportation of textiles and apparel.

The Soviet development strategy stimulated a very high level of economic growth during the early stages of economic development (between 1928 and 1965), because it managed to mobilize all human and financial resources into achieving certain economic objectives. However, between 1965 and 1990 economic growth significantly slowed and even stagnated, as the Soviet policy makers increasingly emphasized large and prestigious projects, ignoring cost effectiveness and overlooking rapid technological changes. In addition, for decades economists and planners often ignored the negative environmental impact of such large projects.

Between 1985 and 1990, the Gorbachev-Ryzhkov administration attempted to repair the most severe economic problems and past mistakes. However, a combination of a cavalier approach to economic management and the incompetence of the administration in implementing reforms led to the malfunctioning of the Soviet economic system in 1990 and 1991.

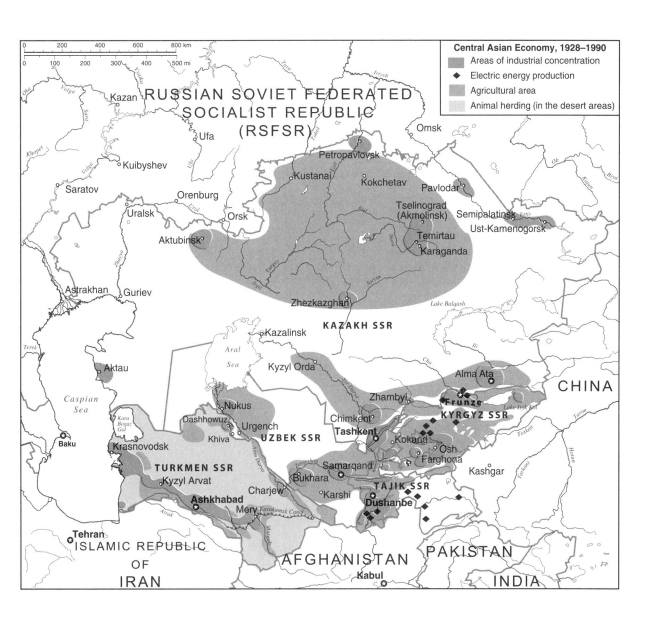

RUSSIAN SOVIET FEDERATED
SOCIALIST REPUBLIC
(RSFSR)

Kazan
Ufa
Kuibyshev
Saratov
Orenburg
Uralsk
Orsk
Aktubinsk
Astrakhan
Guriev
Aktau

Caspian
Sea

Kara
Bogaz
Gol

Baku

Omsk
Petropavlovsk
Kustanai
Kokchetav
Pavlodar
Tselinograd
(Akmolinsk)
Semipalatinsk
Ust-Kamenogorsk
Temirtau
Karaganda
Zhezkazghan

Lake Balqash

KAZAKH SSR

Kazalinsk

Aral
Sea

Kyzyl Orda

Alma Ata

CHINA

Nukus
Dashhowuz
Urgench
Khiva
Krasnovodsk

Zhambyl
Chimkent
Tashkent

Frunze
KYRGYZ SSR

Kokand
Osh
Farghona

Lake Isyk Kol

UZBEK SSR

TURKMEN SSR
Kyzyl Arvat

Samarqand
Bukhara
Karshi

Kashgar

TAJIK SSR
Dushanbe

Charjew
Ashkhabad
Mery
Karakumsk Canal

Tehran
ISLAMIC REPUBLIC
OF
IRAN

AFGHANISTAN
Kabul

PAKISTAN

INDIA

0   200   400   600   800 km
0   100   200   300   400   500 mi

VI

Post-Communism and Independence

Map 40: Interethnic Conflicts and the Collapse of the USSR

Mikhail Gorbachev's policies of *glasnost* and *perestroika* opened up discussions on many issues previously banned by the Soviet authorities. At the same time, however, the democratization process led to political confrontations between supporters and opponents of the reforms, and to the rise of nationalism. It also led to a rapid decline in the legitimacy of existing Soviet institutions without opening opportunities for the creation of new ones. This was especially true in dealings with interethnic and social tensions: The Soviet authorities abandoned the Soviet-era approach of responding to all kinds of tensions exclusively with repression and force, but they did not create new mechanisms for mediating those conflicts and tensions. Thus, the Central Asian republics, like many other parts of the Soviet Union, experienced rising interethnic tensions that sometimes exploded in violent clashes and uprisings. Between 1986 and 1991, interethnic conflicts claimed hundreds, if not thousands, of lives.

Alma Ata (Kazakh SSR). In December 1986 unsanctioned demonstrations in Alma Ata led to clashes between demonstrators and security forces. The immediate cause of the political and ethnic unrest, which later grew into an uprising, was Moscow's order to replace Kazakhstan's leader, Dinmuhammed Kunayev, a native Kazakh, with Gorbachev's protégé, the Russian Gennady Kolbin. Thousands of people gathered in Alma Ata to express their disagreement with the Kremlin's ethnic policy in Kazakhstan in general and with this appointment in particular. The demonstration was brutally put down, mass arrests took place, several people were allegedly killed and several hundred injured. This event led to a sharp ethnic polarization between Kazakhs and Russians, and antagonized Kazakh society.

Ashkhabad and Nebitdag (Turkmen SSR). In May 1989 sporadic riots took place in Turkmenistan's capital city, Ashkhabad, and in the provincial town of Nebitdag. Cars, public buildings and shops (allegedly run by ethnic minorities) were vandalized. The immediate causes of this strife are unknown, though it was believed that the conflicts were products of rising social and interethnic tensions. Although only a few casualties were officially reported, these riots, accompanied in some cases by extremist nationalistic slogans, had a very negative impact and created a nervous atmosphere especially among ethnic minorities.

Novyi Uzen (Kazakh SSR). In 1989 sporadic clashes began between local people and representatives of ethnic minorities employed in the local oil refinery and processing factories. The immediate cause of this mainly communal unrest, localized in a small provincial town, is unknown. It is believed that the degradation of social conditions, growing unemployment and the arrival of a large number of immigrants had led to grievances among the local communities. As a result, the local youth turned against newcomers from the ethnic minorities, who were seen to have jobs, accommodation and social benefits "at the expense" of the local communities.

Farghona (Uzbek SSR). In June 1989 a communal conflict between the Uzbeks and Meskhetian Turks grew into bloody clashes, which spread from the suburbs of the provincial towns of Farghona and Kokand to other cities and towns in the Farghona Valley. According to an official report, over 100 died and 1,000 were injured, and a number of properties, private and public, were destroyed. Tensions were so high and the number killed was so large that there was no option but to relocate the entire community of about 30,000 Meskhetian Turks to Russia.

Dushanbe (Tajik SSR). In February 1990 thousands of people organized a spontaneous demonstration in Dushanbe. The demonstration became violent, with cars, shops and public buildings burned to the ground, and clashes between Tajiks and ethnic minority groups. The immediate cause of this unrest was the news that refugees from Armenia would be relocated to the city. This relocation was allegedly to have been funded by money from the local community budget and houses would supposedly be taken from local low-income families. It is believed that dozens of people were killed during the riots and several hundred were injured. Despite the imposition of a state of emergency and the mobilization of police and army units, sporadic clashes continued for several weeks. As a result, ethnic minorities began leaving Tajikistan: roughly 385,000 people left the country between 1990 and 1992.

Osh-Uzgen (Kyrgyz SSR). In May and June 1990 discord between local communities of Kyrgyzs and Uzbeks turned into mayhem in Uzgen and Osh. The immediate cause of the violence was the news that, in response to the demands of the Kyrgyz movement Osh Aimagy, the local administration was going to distribute plots of land to the landless Kyrgyzs at the expense of the Uzbek community. Protests followed that led to mass clashes between representatives of the two communities. It was the bloodiest event to occur at the time, with official calculations of 220 dead and 1,000 hospitalized (unofficial estimates give figures between 600 and 1,200 killed during the entire disorder).

Against this background of political turmoil and conflicts, the Central Asian republics entered negotiations over the new Soviet Union treaty. This treaty would keep the Soviet Union alive by giving greater autonomy to the Union's republics. However, it awoke serious opposition among the hard-line leaders of the Soviet Union, who attempted a coup d'état in Moscow in August 1991. Although the coup was suppressed, the leaders of three USSR republics, Russia, the Ukraine and Byelorussia, signed an agreement that unconditionally dissolved the USSR in December of 1991.

Map 41: Independent Kazakhstan

On 16 December 1991 Kazakhstan declared its independence from the Soviet Union. Its regional importance was enhanced by the fact that the country of about 15.3 million people—the second most populous in Central Asia (2007 CIA est.)—has the largest territory in the region and is the ninth largest in the world. It has historically been one of the most ethnically diverse countries in the region, including Kazakhs (64.4 percent), Russians (20.0 percent), Ukrainians (3.7), Uzbeks (2.5), Germans (2.4), Tatars (1.7) and others (5.3) (2007 official est.). Since 1991 a significant number of Russians and Germans have left the country. During Kazakhstan's first decade of independence there was a great deal of concern about secessionist movements in the northern provinces of the country and about interethnic tensions in the south (see map 40). These concerns were largely put to rest in the early 2000s, due to the changing demographic balance in Kazakhstan.

The Kazakhstan government responded to the social, economic and security challenges by adopting policies that combined political and economic liberalizations with the retention of certain forms of direct and indirect state control over aspects of people's lives. Opposition political parties and independent media were permitted, as long as they did not directly challenge the government and its policies. President Nursultan Nazarbayev, who served as prime minister between 1984 and 1989 and was first elected president in 1990, has ruled the country without interruption for nearly two decades. In December 2005 Nazarbayev was reelected to the presidency for a seven-year term.

In the early 1990s Kazakhstan's leaders attempted to present the country as an "economic tiger of Central Asia," believing that enormous reserves of natural resources, especially oil, plus an advanced industrial sector and a well-educated population would create momentum for fast and dynamic economic development. From the Soviet era Kazakhstan had inherited a well-diversified economy in which the oil-extracting sectors, with a highly developed transportation infrastructure of pipelines and railroads, played a key role.

Despite possessing huge natural resources and a small population, Kazakhstan experienced a severe economic recession in the 1990s. The government selectively accepted an IMF-designed program of radical economic changes and opened the country to the forces of globalization. It approved mass privatization, price liberalization and currency reforms, allowed private entrepreneurship and free trade. At the same time it retained some degree of regulation and control over the so-called strategic sectors of the national economy. A national currency—Kazakhstan's *tenge*—was introduced in 1993 and was openly exchanged for all major currencies, although it took a while to achieve full convertibility. Annual inflation fluctuated between 600 and 1,200 percent between 1993 and 1998, but the country achieved some degree of macroeconomic stabilization in the 2000s and the annual inflation rate declined to 8.6 percent (2007 CIA est.).

Economic changes and globalization brought winners and losers. Between 1990 and 1999 Kazakhstan's economy experienced a steep decline, especially in the agricultural and manufacturing sectors. However, the country attracted significant direct foreign investment into its oil, gas and nonferrous metal-extracting sectors, becoming one of the leading destinations for investors in the region by the 2000s. The government invested a large portion of its oil revenue in infrastructure, transportation and construction, and created special funds to accumulate oil revenue windfalls for future generations.

Industry and services are the two main pillars of Kazakhstan's post-Soviet national economy, contributing 39.5 and 53.7 percent respectively to GDP in 2005 (2007 World Bank est.); the agricultural sector remains important in terms of employment though it produces only 6.8 percent of GDP. Exports are still narrowly based on sales of raw materials on international markets. The country's main exports are oil (in 2006 it produced 65 million tons of oil or 1.3 million barrels a day), gas (25.6 billion cubic meters), textiles, grain, cotton and other agricultural products (2007 Economist Intelligence Unit est.). The government's target is to double the country's GDP within the next ten to fifteen years, which would put Kazakhstan among the world's top 50 most developed nations.

In the 1990s Kazakhstan experienced a steady decline in living standards across all groups of the population, with the exception of a very small number of people who benefited from market opportunities. The 2000s brought a rapid increase in living standards. As of 2007 Kazakhstan has the highest per capita income in the region and the second highest among CIS members. In 2006 the UN Development Program's Human Development Index (HDI) ranked Kazakhstan in 79th place out of 177, on a par with Saudi Arabia, the Ukraine and Lebanon. Unlike other Central Asian republics, Kazakhstan became a net receiver of large-scale economic migration (the second most in the CIS, and the ninth most popular destination for immigrants in the world).

Between 2002 and 2008 Kazakhstan received huge inflows of oil revenue due to rapidly rising oil prices on the international market and completion of several oil projects and pipelines. During this period it experienced robust economic growth, averaging between 7 and 11 percent annually, due to favorable conditions in the domestic and international markets. Kazakhstan became the only country in the former USSR to move its capital to a new location: the government moved from Almaty to the city of Astana in 1997.

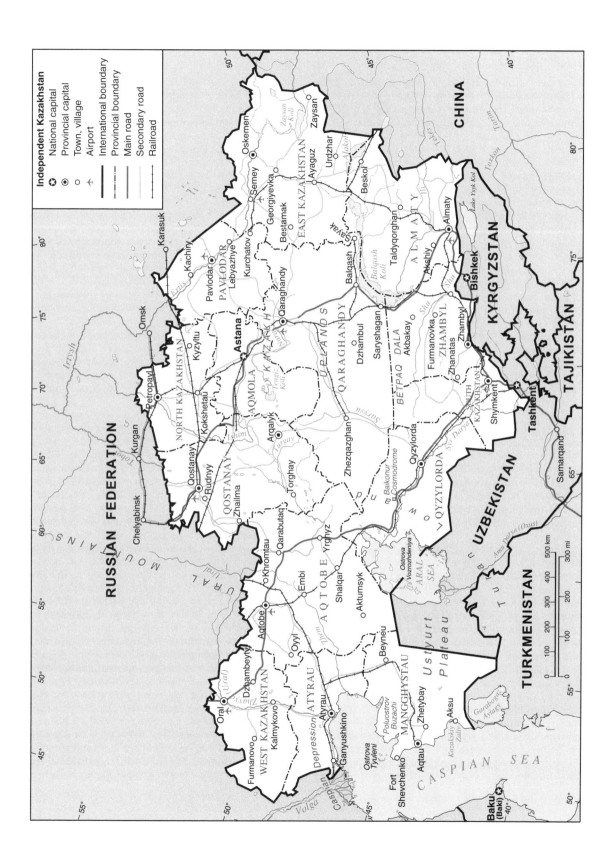

Independent Kazakhstan

- ✪ National capital
- ◉ Provincial capital
- ○ Town, village
- ✈ Airport
- ——— International boundary
- —··— Provincial boundary
- ——— Main road
- ——— Secondary road
- ——— Railroad

RUSSIAN FEDERATION

CHINA

KYRGYZSTAN

TAJIKISTAN

UZBEKISTAN

TURKMENISTAN

CASPIAN SEA

ARAL SEA

Astana

Bishkek

Tashkent

Baku (Baki)

Karasuk
Omsk
Kurgan
Chelyabinsk
Petropavl
Qostanay
Rudnyy
Zhailma
Qarabutaq
Khromtau
Aqtobe
Oyyl
Dzhambeyty
Furmanovo
Oral
Kalmykovo
Atyrau
Ganyushkino
Fort Shevchenko
Aqtau
Aksu
Zhetybay
Beyneu
Shalqar
Aktumsyk
Embi
Yrghyz
Qaraghandy
Arqalyk
Torghay
Zhezqazghan
Kokshetau
Kyzyltu
Pavlodar
Lebyazhye
Kachiry
Oskemen
Semey
Georgiyevka
Zaysan
Ayaguz
Urdzhar
Beskol
Bestamak
Kurchatov
Sayak
Balqash
Taldyqorghan
Almaty
Akshiy
Zhambyl
Zhanatas
Furmanovka
Akbakay
Dzhambul
Saryshagan
Shymkent
Qyzylorda
Baikonur Cosmodrome
Samarqand

EAST KAZAKHSTAN
NORTH KAZAKHSTAN
PAVLODAR
AQMOLA
QOSTANAY
WEST KAZAKHSTAN
ATYRAU
MANGGHYSTAU
AQTOBE
QARAGHANDY
ALMATY
ZHAMBYL
SOUTH KAZAKHSTAN
QYZYLORDA

URAL MOUNTAINS
KAZAKH UPLANDS
BETPAQ DALA
Ustyurt Plateau
Poluostrov Buzachi
Ostrova Tyuleni
Ostrova Vozrozhdeniya
Kazakskiy Zaliv
Garabogaz Aylagy

Zaysan Koli
Balqash Koli
Tengiz Koli
Lake Ysyk Kol

Irtysh
Tobol
Ural
Ishim
Turgay
Sarysu
Shu
Syr Darya
Zhayyq
Amu Darya (Oxus)
Volga
Toxqan
Tarim
Ili
Alakol

0	100	200	300	400	500 km
0	100	200	300 mi		

Map 42: Independent Kyrgyzstan

Kyrgyzstan declared its independence from the USSR on 31 August 1991. The country of about 4.5 million people embarked on its independence against a background of serious interethnic conflicts (see map 40). At the time of independence, ethnic Kyrgyzs accounted for less then 52 percent of the total population (1999 census). However, changes in the ethnic balance and numerous political, cultural and social concessions saw tensions ease by the late 1990s. Yet, in the 1990s a significant number of Russians and representatives of various minority groups left the country. By 2007 the country's population was 5.3 million but it had become far less diverse and far more stable, with Kyrgyzs accounting for 68 percent of the population, Uzbeks 13.8 percent, Russians 9.5 percent, Dungans (Muslim Chinese) 1.1 percent and others 7.6 percent (2007 est.).

Kyrgyzstan established the most liberal regime in the region under President Askar Akayev. Akayev won the presidential elections in 1990, competing against a powerful Communist Party leader. He opened the doors for opposition political parties, independent media and NGOs, and cooperated with international organizations by experimenting with political reforms. These measures ultimately won his country the title "Island of Democracy." By the end of the 1990s, however, the situation had radically changed. Akayev began increasingly to rely on his family members, cronies and regional-based clans to run the country. The corrupt and intolerant regime persecuted its critics and jailed the most radical opposition leaders and journalists. In 1995 and again in 2000 Akayev won presidential elections by large margins, but many independent observers leveled accusations that these elections were unfair and rigged. In March 2005 grievances and dissatisfaction caused by corruption, mismanagement and cronyism led to mass unrest and ultimately resulted in the "Tulip (Yellow) Revolution." Akayev and his family fled the country. In July 2005 Kurmanbek Bakiyev was elected president for a five-year term. The new president promised to conduct a series of political reforms including constitutional changes, and to fight corruption and cronyism. However, he too was accused of cronyism and corruption, and several opposition parties organized mass demonstrations in 2006 and 2007 demanding his resignation.

Throughout the 1990s Kyrgyzstan was the only country in Central Asia to fully embrace the so-called Shock Therapy approach in economic reform prescribed by the IMF and World Bank. It introduced radical market and trade liberalization, mass privatization and structural reforms. Despite all these reforms and considerable international assistance, Kyrgyzstan's economy suffered a deep, decade-long recession. According to the World Bank, the country's economy declined at an average annual rate of between 5 and 8 percent from 1990 to 2000. It succeeded in attracting foreign direct investments to its natural resources–extracting sector only, especially to its gold-mining sector. Foreign investors have been reluctant to invest in other sectors because of the amount of red tape imposed by the national bureaucracy and the small size of the local market.

Kyrgyzstan's national currency—the *som*—was introduced in May 1993. Annual inflation fluctuated between 300 and 1,200 percent between 1991 and 1995, and the national economy was negatively affected by Asian and Russian financial crises in 1997 and 1998. Macroeconomic stabilization was achieved in the early 2000s and the annual inflation rate was brought under control, settling at a relatively low level and fluctuating between 2 and 6 percent (2007 CIA est.).

Agriculture, industry and services are the three main pillars of post-Soviet Kyrgyzstan's economy, contributing 34.5, 19.5 and 46 percent respectively to GDP in 2006 (2006, CIA est.). Exports are narrowly based on sales of raw materials on the international market. The country's main exports are gold, textiles, tobacco, raw cotton and other agricultural products (2007 EIU est.). Kyrgyzstan has accumulated the highest external debt per capita in the Central Asian region.

The post-Soviet economic changes have led to a steady decline in living standards among all sections of Kyrgyzstan's population, despite the recent macroeconomic stabilization. The country remains one of the poorest of the former Soviet Union, with 40 percent of its people living below the poverty line (2007 CIA est.) and an average life expectancy of 67.1 years (2006 UNDP est.). In 2006 the UN Development Program's Human Development Index (HDI) put Kyrgyzstan in 110th place out of 177, on a par with Syria, Egypt and Vietnam. Due to mass poverty and the economic recession, a large number of Kyrgyz citizens have emigrated from the country in the post-Soviet era. In the first wave, about a half-million of the Russian-speaking population left the country in the first half of the 1990s. In addition, between 300,000 and 700,000 ethnic Kyrgyzs have moved to Russia, Kazakhstan and other destinations in search of jobs and economic opportunities since 1997–1998. It is estimated that these economic migrants send to their home country the equivalent of 200 or 300 million U.S. dollars annually in remittances.

Like the other Central Asian states, between 2002 and 2007 Kyrgyzstan experienced economic growth, although at a very slow rate, between 0.5 and 3.5 percent annually on average. By 2006–2007, neighboring Kazakhstan had become one of the largest investors in Kyrgyzstan, focusing mainly on the construction and financial sectors and infrastructure projects.

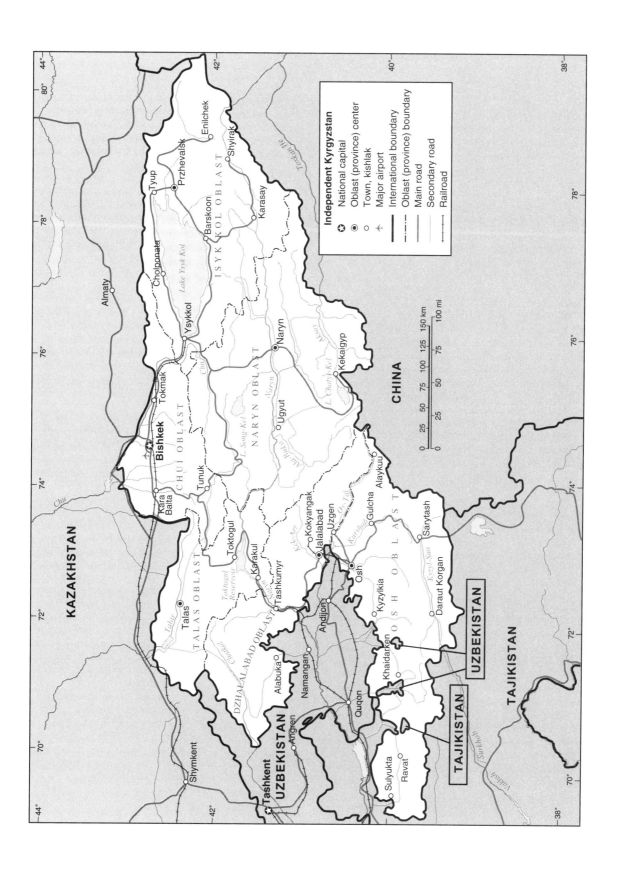

Map 43: Independent Tajikistan

Tajikistan declared its independence from the Soviet Union on 9 September 1991. The country entered independence as one of the poorest states in the region. Its population was growing at the fastest rate in the former USSR—32.65 births per 1,000 people (2006 CIA est.)—doubling every 20 to 25 years and thus creating enormous pressure on the fragile environment of the mountains that occupy about 90 percent of its territory. The Tajiks account for 79.9 percent of the population, Uzbeks 15.3, Russians and others about 4.8 percent. Though Tajikistan had built a relatively well-diversified economy and experienced high economic growth from the 1930s through the 1970s, it experienced economic stagnation and slow growth throughout the 1980s. On the eve of independence Tajik society was in turmoil due to widespread social unrest, interethnic tensions and political confrontations.

In the early 1990s the political scene was dominated by three groups. The Communist Party of Tajikistan (CPT) and its successors tried to retain tight control over the political system and economy. The radical nationalist opposition demanded significant changes and reforms, including the removal of the CPT from power, while its ultranationalist wing demanded the revision of existing borders and claimed that important cities with significant Tajik-speaking populations such as Bukhara and Samarqand should be transferred from Uzbekistan to Tajikistan. Small but very active groups of Islamic activists also emerged, who worked under the umbrella of, or in cooperation with, the Islamic Party of Renaissance (Tajikistan) (IPRT).

The CPT won the parliamentary elections in 1990 and its representative, Rahmon Nabyev, won the presidential election, but the opposition refused to recognize the results. In 1992 a civil war, fueled by regional rivalry and growing Islamic radicalism, broke out in Tajikistan, leading to the ouster of President Nabyev. After numerous clashes in which both sides—the government and the opposition—destroyed infrastructure, property and irrigation systems, a coalition of the regional elite installed Imomali Rakhmonov as head of the parliament. In 1994 he won the presidential election. The opposition, united under the umbrella of the United Tajik Opposition (UTO), established control over most provinces but failed to capture the capital. In 1997, with UN, Russian and Iranian assistance, Rakhmonov managed to negotiate and sign a peace accord with the UTO. The accord granted the UTO a fixed share of positions in the government and free participation in parliamentary elections. In bitterly contested presidential elections in 1999 and in 2006, the UTO candidate lost to President Rakhmonov.

The civil war had a devastating effect on the national economy. According to the World Bank, Tajikistan's economy declined at an average annual rate of 6–7 percent between 1990 and 2000. Practically all manufacturing plants were closed due to political and economic instability, high inflation and lack of investment. However, the natural resources extracting sector survived, as it received considerable government support and investment. With the end of the civil war in 1997, Tajikistan's government adopted a program of postwar economic reconstruction focusing on the restoration of major sectors of the economy and achieving self-efficiency in food provision. The government gradually liberalized its trade, opened the national economy to international investment and introduced its own national currency, the *somoni*, in October 2000.

Agriculture, industry and services are the three main pillars of modern Tajikistan's economy, contributing 23.4, 28.6 and 48.0 percent respectively to GDP (2006 World Bank est.). The country depends heavily on imports of machinery, oil, gas, industrial consumer goods and food products; it increasingly relies on the export of raw materials to the international market, especially aluminum, silver, electricity, cotton and fruits. After 1991 Tajikistan became one of the major routes for illicit drugs (especially opium) transiting from Afghanistan to Russia and further to Eastern and Western Europe. The advent of large-scale drug smuggling has contributed to the rise of a shadow economy that accounts for nearly 40 percent of the country's GDP.

Tajikistan's total external debt reached 773.2 million U.S. dollars in 2004 (2004 World Bank est.) and is expected to grow further in the near future. The country needs considerable foreign direct investment and international assistance to modernize existing technologies and to implement major economic changes.

Due to the civil war and the difficulties of postwar reconciliation, there has been a steady decline in living standards among the population, especially among women and children. In 2006 the UN Development Program's Human Development Index (HDI) put Tajikistan in 122nd place out of 177, down from 34th place in 1991. The country remains the poorest in the former Soviet Union, with average monthly wages ranging from 18 to 30 U.S. dollars and with 64 percent of the population living below the poverty line (2007 EIU est.). It is estimated that between 70,000 and 110,000 people left Tajikistan annually in the 1990s for Russia, Kazakhstan and other countries in search of jobs and better standards of living.

Between 2002 and 2008, however, Tajikistan experienced robust annual economic growth of 7 to 8 percent due to favorable conditions in domestic and international markets. Significant rises in commodity prices on the international market boosted the state's revenue. Tajikistan also attracted significant foreign investment in the energy and construction sectors of its economy. In addition, large sums in the form of remittances, estimated at between 200 and 500 million U.S. dollars per annum, were sent to Tajikistan by Tajiks working in other countries.

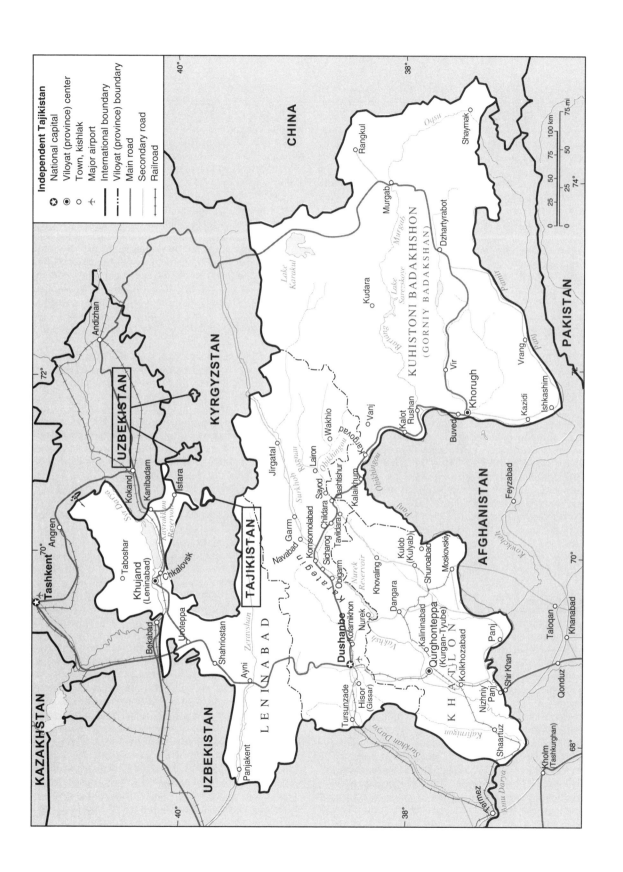

Map 44: Independent Turkmenistan

On 27 October 1991 Turkmenistan declared its independence from the USSR. The country of about 5.1 million people embarked on its independence under very favorable conditions. It possesses enormous reserves of natural gas and significant reserves of oil, which stirred speculation that Turkmenistan would be the Kuwait of Central Asia. From the Soviet era Turkmenistan inherited a relatively diversified economy, in which the gas- and oil-extracting sectors along with a well-developed transportation infrastructure (including export-oriented pipelines) played key roles. Its society is one the most homogeneous in the region, as Turkmens account for 85 percent of the population, Russians about 4 percent, Uzbeks about 5 percent, and others about 6 percent (2007 est.). Since 1991 a significant number of Russians and Russian-speaking groups have left the country.

Post-independence reforms in Turkmenistan have brought to life one of the most extreme political regimes in the former USSR. Saparmurat Niyazov was elected president in 1990 and requested that he be called Turkmenbashy (father of all Turkmen). He introduced a national policy represented by the slogan "Khalq, Vatan, Turkmenbashy!" (People, Fatherland, Turkmenbashy). In 1999 the Mejlis (parliament) endorsed him as president for life. But in December 2006 he unexpectedly died, allegedly of heart failure, and in February 2007 his successor, Gurbanguly Berdymukhammedov, was elected president for a five-year term. The political system in Turkmenistan combines extreme forms of statism, egalitarianism, and authoritarianism with nationalism and emphasis on traditional values. The Communist Party of Turkmenistan was renamed the Democratic Party of Turkmenistan (DPT) in December 1991 and has remained the sole ruling party (as of 2007). All major opposition parties were banned and a significant number of Turkmen political leaders went into exile, mainly to Russia, Norway and Sweden. In addition, the Turkmen government established tight control over the media, banning all independent media outlets and even imposing state control over Internet access. In 2007 Berdymukhammedov promised to conduct some political reforms, including political and economic liberalization.

Despite possessing vast natural resources and having only a small population, the economic achievements of Turkmenistan in the post-Soviet era have been mixed. The Turkmenistan government rejected an IMF-designed program of radical economic changes, confident that the sale of the country's gas reserves—which they believed to be among the largest in the world—would allow Turkmenistan to become prosperous within 10 to 15 years. The government approved small-scale privatization, limited price liberalization and currency reforms, allowed private entrepreneurship and selectively liberalized trade. But at the same time, it retained a form of centrally planned economy and control over most of the enterprises in the industrial and agricultural sectors. The national currency, the *manta*, was introduced in November 1993. After a turbulent period from 1992 to 1998 during which annual inflation fluctuated between 600 and 3,000 percent, the country managed to reduce the inflation rate to 11 percent (2007 CIA est.).

Despite its apparent advantages, Turkmenistan's economic miracle did not materialize. This was largely due to three factors: nonpayments for gas by the CIS partners; the absence of a gas pipeline to the non-CIS market; and the weaknesses of the economic development model chosen by Turkmenistan's leaders. According to the World Bank, Turkmenistan's economy declined at an average annual rate of 4.8 percent between 1990 and 2000. The country failed to attract sizable direct foreign investment to modernize its gas and oil extracting facilities or to build new pipelines (see map 49).

Agriculture, industry and services are the three main pillars of post-Soviet Turkmenistan's economy, contributing 17.7, 39.2 and 43.2 percent respectively to GDP in 2006 (2006, CIA est.). Exports are narrowly based on sales of raw materials on the international markets. The country's main exports are gas (in 2007 the country exported 58,000 million cubic meters of gas), oil (5.5 million tons exported), textiles, cotton (Turkmenistan is the world's tenth largest producer of cotton), silk and other agricultural products (2007 EIU est.).

The economic changes introduced in the 1990s have led to a decade of steady decline in living standards among all groups of the population, despite the fact that the state provides water, electricity and gas free to all citizens, and despite, too, some recent macroeconomic stabilization. The country's healthcare, education and social welfare systems deteriorated significantly and an average life expectancy dropped to 62.5 years (2006 UNDP est.). In 2006 the UN Development Program's Human Development Index (HDI) put Turkmenistan in 105th place out of 177, on a par with El Salvador, Algeria and Jamaica. Unlike other Central Asian republics, Turkmenistan has not experienced a large-scale economic migration of its population during the post-Soviet era.

Between 2002 and 2008 Turkmenistan experienced robust economic growth of 7 to 12 percent annually due to favorable conditions in domestic and international markets. A significant rise in the prices of commodities on the international market boosted the state's revenue. A renegotiation of terms for gas and oil deliveries to Russia and the Ukraine significantly increased state revenues between 2002 and 2007. And yet, Turkmenistan's agricultural sector and transportation infrastructure, especially pipelines, are run-down and require substantial investment and improvements.

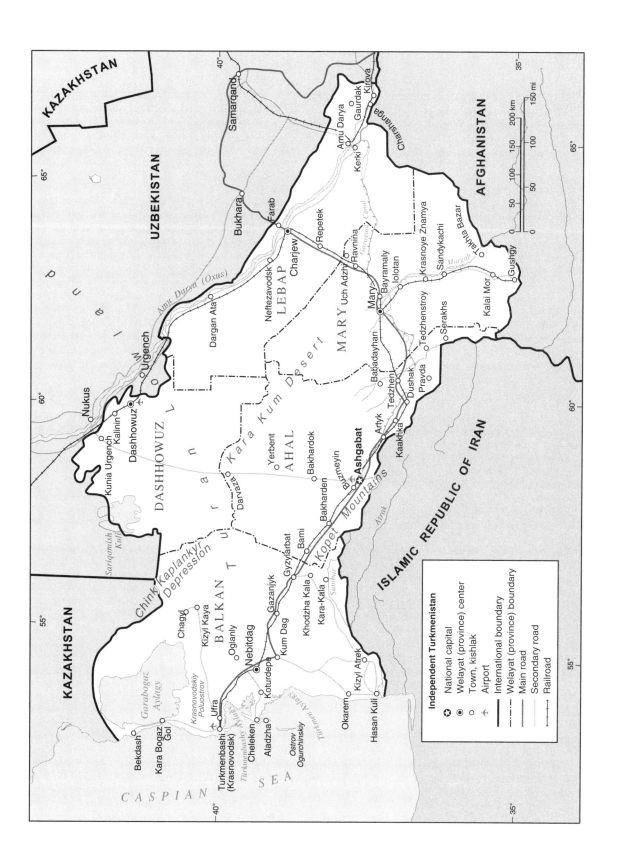

Map 45: Independent Uzbekistan

Uzbekistan officially declared its independence from the USSR on 1 September 1991. The country began its independence against a background of rising social tensions and a looming ecological crisis. The country has about 27.8 million people (2007 CIA est.), making it the largest in the region in terms of population. The population is very young, with about 50 percent below the age of 25. The population could double within the next 25 to 30 years if the current birth rate remains unchanged. The rapidly growing population puts enormous pressure on the country's environment and natural resources, with about half of its territory experiencing a severe shortage of drinking water. In addition, large land areas face salinization and desertification.

Uzbekistan's society has long been relatively homogeneous, with ethnic Uzbeks accounting for 80 percent of the population, Tajiks about 5 percent, Russians about 5.5 percent, Kazakhs about 3 percent, Karakalpaks 2.5 percent, Tatars 1.5 percent and others 2.5 percent (2007 est.). Since 1991 a significant number of Russians and Russian-speaking groups have left the country due to interethnic tensions and uncertainty about their future.

Citing political instability, the rise of social unrest, Islamic radicalism and interethnic tensions, Uzbekistan has been slow to conduct political reforms. The government developed policies emphasizing egalitarianism, traditional community values, nationalism and the central role of the state and state institutions in regulating and controlling the country's political processes. The Communist Party of Uzbekistan was renamed the People's Democratic Party (PDP) in 1991 and continued playing an important role in Uzbekistan's political life. All major opposition political parties were banned and their leaders were persecuted or went into exile. The government also established tight control over the media, banning all independent media outlets. In 1990 and again in 2000, Islam Karimov was elected president (he skipped elections in 1995, as his term in office was extended by a popular referendum).

Uzbekistan inherited from the Soviet era a well-developed and well-diversified economy; however, its restructuring and reforming proved very difficult. The government initially turned to the international expertise of the World Bank, IMF, European Bank of Reconstruction and Development, Asian Development Bank and others, though it outright rejected the Shock Therapy approach. By the mid-1990s it had devised the so-called Uzbekistan Model of Development that emphasized gradual reforms, gradual privatization and liberalization and the preservation of the state's central role in controlling the national economy. Although the government approved small-scale privatization, allowed private entrepreneurship and conducted currency reforms, at the same time it retained a form of centrally planned economy, large-scale subsidies and direct control over the industrial and agricultural sectors. The national currency, the *sum*, was introduced in 1993. A currency black market emerged due to the state's strict control over the convertibility of the *sum*. After a turbulent period from 1993 to 2001, during which annual inflation fluctuated between 400 and 3,000 percent, in the early 2000s the country achieved some degree of macroeconomic stability, with an annual official inflation rate of 7.6 percent in 2006 (2007 CIA est.).

During the 1990s Uzbekistan's approach to economic reform helped it avoid a steep economic recession, mass closure of factories and plants and the mass unemployment seen in many neighboring Central Asian states. Uzbekistan even attracted direct foreign investment in its resources-extracting sectors, especially gold extraction and processing, nonferrous metals and textiles, and in its manufacturing sector—it became the first country in the region to begin producing cars (at a joint Uzbek-Korean plant). By the late 1990s, however, foreign investors were becoming reluctant to invest in the economy due to the continued inconvertibility of the national currency and the state's centralized economic controls.

Agriculture, industry and services are the three main pillars of post-Soviet Uzbekistan's economy, contributing 31.1, 25.7 and 43.2 percent respectively to GDP in 2005 (2006, CIA est.). The country's exports to the international market include cotton (it is the region's largest producer), gold (it is the third largest producer in the CIS), energy products, textiles and some machinery. Due to macroeconomic difficulties and huge spending on the social welfare system and on various large projects, Uzbekistan has accumulated about 4.7 billion U.S. dollars in external debt, the largest in the region (2007 CIA est.).

Uzbekistan experienced a steady decline in living standards among all groups of the population in the 1990s. The country remains one of the poorest countries of the former Soviet Union, with 33 percent of the population living below the poverty line (2007 CIA est.). In 2006 the UN Development Program's Human Development Index (HDI) put Uzbekistan in 113th place out of 177, on a par with Egypt and Nicaragua. As in some other Central Asian republics, a large number of economic migrants left Uzbekistan in the post-Soviet era.

Between 2002 and 2008 Uzbekistan experienced annual economic growth between 4 and 7 percent, due to favorable conditions on the domestic and international markets. A significant rise in the prices of international market commodities boosted the state's revenues and Uzbekistan managed to improve its trade with partners in the region and in the CIS. Yet, the country failed to attract significant foreign investment in its economy; its transportation infrastructure, energy facilities and agriculture have become run-down and require substantial investment and improvements.

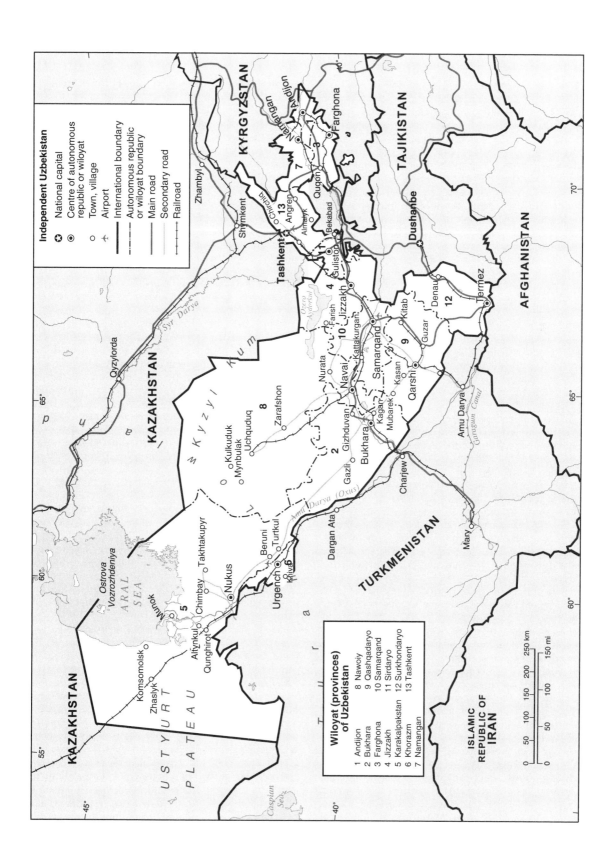

Map 46: Ethnic Composition and Major Territorial Disputes

The post-Soviet era's interethnic problems and major territorial disputes were very much a product of the USSR's so-called nationality policies. From 1924 to 1926 the Soviet authorities conducted their nation-state delimitation in the region (see map 37), and over the next six decades they supported the development of all the attributes of the modern nation—national vernacular language and mass literacy, national identity associated with territory and various national symbols. Communist government officials believed that national identity and nationalism would inevitably give way to "socialist internationalism." In this political philosophy, the borders between the Central Asian Soviet republics played merely symbolic administrative roles, though the external borders were sealed by the "iron curtain" and reinforced by the military might of the Soviet state.

The dissolution of the USSR brought significant changes in relations both among the Central Asian republics and with the outside world. Suddenly the issue of ethnic minorities and the demarcation of borders became very important. Four major problems connected to borders and ethnicity seriously undermined relations between the countries, problems which, if not effectively addressed, had the potential to provoke major regional wars.

First, the Soviet-era borders often divided ethnic communities, sometimes literally cutting through towns and villages, for those borders were in fact largely irrelevant before 1991. In the case of the Farghona Valley, for example, as of 1991 up to half a million Uzbeks remained in Kyrgyzstan and Tajikistan, while several hundred thousand Tajiks and thousands of Kyrgyzs lived in Uzbekistan.

Second, suzerainty and capitalist materialism brought fierce competition for natural resources in many border districts. In the past, the Soviet government had regulated distribution of water, roads and energy infrastructure so as to be equally shared between the communities on both sides of any given border. In the post-Soviet era, nothing could stop one community from monopolizing resources or infrastructure.

Third, some communities laid so-called historical claims on the territories of neighboring states, citing historical evidence and the precolonial distribution of political power, culture and ethnic groups. Certain Tajik groups, for instance, claimed that Bukhara and Samarqand should belong to the Tajik state as they were traditionally Tajik centers of culture and learning, while some Uzbek activists demanded that the Kyrgyz cities of Osh and Uzgen should belong to Uzbekistan.

Fourth, the problem of ethnic separatism emerged in many areas of the region. For example, several million ethnic Russians had been living in the northern districts and provinces of Kazakhstan for many generations, while many ethnic Kazakhs lived in the border provinces in the Russian Federation. About one million Uzbeks live in the border districts in each of the neighboring Central Asian states, while a significant number of Tajiks live in Uzbekistan and Kyrgyzstan.

In addition, Kazakhstan, Kyrgyzstan and Tajikistan inherited from the Russian colonial and Soviet eras territorial disputes with the People's Republic of China (PRC). Territorial disputes with Afghanistan emerged as well, and the Amu Darya River, traditionally accepted in some areas as the border between Afghanistan and Tajikistan and Uzbekistan, was gradually changing its course due to natural causes and climatic changes.

Overall, experts on the region identified between 30 and 60 conflicting points and disputed areas in the border territories of Central Asia. These border issues and claims were often championed by radical nationalist groups, thus seriously undermining relations between the newly independent states.

While the Central Asian republics chose different approaches to deal with each individual case, some common ground was agreed upon. The initial framework for settling interethnic problems and border disputes within the region was set up by the Almaty Declaration in December 1991. The declaration guaranteed the political and cultural rights of the ethnic minorities in every republic in the region, with each government pledging not to discriminate against any ethnic groups. It was also affirmed that all signatories of the declaration would recognize existing borders and abstain from territorial claims upon each other.

The demarcation of borders started in 1992 and 1993, and major border revisions were completed between 1997 and 2007 when appropriate bilateral treaties were signed. All the Central Asian states except Uzbekistan opted to keep the borders demilitarized, and only in 1993–1994 did they establish checkpoints on the main roads. The government of Uzbekistan chose a different approach, and decided to introduce Soviet-style control over its borders by not only establishing checkpoints and installing barbed wire but also creating minefields along some stretches.

Border disputes between the PRC on the one hand and Kazakhstan, Kyrgyzstan, Tajikistan and Russia on the other were settled on a multilateral basis within the framework of the Shanghai Cooperation Organization (SCO), established in April 1996. SCO's main purpose was to resolve territorial disputes and to demilitarize borders. All border disputes between China, Kazakhstan, Kyrgyzstan and Tajikistan were officially settled by 1998 and 1999, with the parties signing agreements on borders and demilitarization. Some nationalistic elements in Kyrgyzstan used the secret nature of the negotiations and the fact that Kyrgyzstan transferred several hundred hectares of land to Chinese jurisdiction as a pretext to criticize President Askar Akayev for "selling out his fatherland."

Territorial Disputes	
	Border disputes in Farghona Valley
Uzgen	Cities claimed by neighboring countries
	Areas of concentrated minority populations
	Border conflicts with China

RUSSIAN FEDERATION

Kazan

Ufa

Kuibyshev

Omsk

Petropavl

Saratov

Orenburg

Qostanai

Kokshetau

Pavlodar

Oral

Orsk

Astana

Semei

Oskemen

Aktube

Temirtau

Qaragandy

Astrakhan

Atyrau

Zhezqazghan

KAZAKHSTAN

Balqash

Aktau

Qazali

Lake Balqash

Caspian
Sea

Aral
Sea

Qyzylorda

Ili

Taldyqorgan

Kara
Bogaz
Gol

Nukus

Dashhowuz

Urgench

Zhambyl

Chu

Almaty

CHINA

Khiva

Shimkent

Tashkent

Bishkek

Lake Ysyk Kol

UZBEKISTAN

KYRGYZSTAN

Baku

AZERBAIJAN

Turkmenbashi

Uzgen

Osh

Kashgar

Tarim

Nebitdag

TURKMENISTAN

Charjew

Samarqand
Bukhara

Farghona

Gyzylarbat

Ashgabat

Qarshi

Dushanbe

TAJIKISTAN

Mary

Karakumsk Canal

Tehran

ISLAMIC REPUBLIC
OF
IRAN

AFGHANISTAN

PAKISTAN

Kabul

INDIA

Map 47: Central Asia and the War on International Terrorism

The Central Asian republics showed remarkable political stability after the collapse of communism in 1991, in sharp contrast to Yugoslavia or Afghanistan after the Soviet occupation. The only country in the region to experience significant turmoil in the 1990s was Tajikistan, and even there the conflict was quickly contained. Beneath this perceived stability, however, a very complex situation has emerged wherein a number of small and dynamic groups and networks are prepared to challenge the ruling regimes.

From the first years of independence all national governments faced small radical and terrorist groups. Uzbekistan and Tajikistan took very harsh measures against some radical critics and opponents, denying them political participation. This harsh approach in turn provoked a backlash, as young people with no opportunity for political participation were increasingly drawn into the ranks of extremist groups. Among the most visible and potentially the strongest were the radical Islamic organizations, some of which gradually rose in size and sophistication, becoming components of various international networks of terrorist groups.

In response to these challenges and rising tensions, all the Central Asian republics banned any political organizations based on religious or ethnic ideologies or programs. Among the outlawed organizations were several small groups that demanded enforcement of stricter Islamic moral norms and eventually the introduction of Shariah, the Islamic legal system. Some of these groups were dismantled by law enforcement agencies, others moved underground or began working at community levels, and some migrated to other countries in search of support.

The civil war in Tajikistan from 1992 to 1997 opened a new chapter in the development of radical political groups that were increasingly attracted by extreme Islamic ideologies. Many individuals from different parts of the region traveled to Tajikistan to participate in the war as "warriors of faith" (*mujahedin*) supporting various Islamic groups. After a series of defeats, the *mujahedin* and many members of the Tajik opposition moved into Afghanistan. According to a number of estimates, between 20,000 and 100,000 Central Asians found refuge in Afghanistan. It was during this period that Central Asian political activists first established contact with the Taliban movement, and probably also with the Al-Qaida organization.

In the late 1990s some of these young activists began returning to their home countries in the region and organizing themselves into more active political networks and groups. In those years two major radical Islamic groups emerged in the region: the Islamic Movement of Uzbekistan (IMU) and Hizb-ut-Tahrir.

The Islamic Movement of Uzbekistan established its power base in the Tajikistan parts of the Farghona Valley, but recruited its members from Kyrgyzstan and Uzbekistan. The IMU's ultimate goal has been to overthrow Islam Karimov's political regime in Uzbekistan by force and to establish an Islamic state. Several times in 1999, 2000 and 2001, the IMU launched high-profile attacks into Uzbekistan from their Tajikistan bases via Kyrgyzstan territory. On one occasion the group even captured and held a number of small towns in Kyrgyzstan for several weeks but were repelled by the Kyrgyz army with help from Uzbek, Russian and Kazakh forces. A series of suicide bombings that shook the capital of Uzbekistan in spring 2004 were allegedly masterminded by the IMU.

Hizb-ut-Tahrir established its power base in the Farghona Valley, but it is claimed to have a strong presence in all Central Asian republics. Its ultimate goal is also to establish an Islamic state, but the activists of the organization have often stated that they would like to achieve their goal by peaceful means.

Both groups have a history of prominent activism in the region. They both appear to have close relations with the Taliban and Al-Qaida, and they are believed to be involved in illicit drug trafficking. Neither allegation, however, has ever been documented.

The situation changed drastically after the September 11, 2001, attack on the United States and the ensuing war in Afghanistan. The Central Asian governments lost no time in condemning the terrorist actions and joined the U.S.-led efforts to overthrow the Taliban regime in Afghanistan. All the Central Asian republics granted overflight rights in their airspace to the U.S. and NATO aircraft involved in humanitarian and rescue operations and air-support for the ground troops in Afghanistan. Three of the Central Asian republics—Kyrgyzstan, Tajikistan and Uzbekistan—agreed to host U.S. and NATO military personnel on their territory. Subsequently, in early 2002 the U.S.-led coalition established two military airbases in the region. One was at Manas airport in Kyrgyzstan (still operational as of 2007); the other was at Hanabad Airport in Uzbekistan. Several military facilities in Tajikistan have been used by U.S. and NATO troops for a variety of missions.

With the beginning of the war in Iraq, however, relations between the Central Asian governments and the United States deteriorated. Although Kazakhstan sent military engineers to Iraq and pledged to keep them in the country "as long as there is a need," other republics were reluctant to lend their unconditional support for the war. In addition, Russia and China put pressure on Kyrgyzstan and Uzbekistan over the U.S. military bases, demanding a clear deadline for their closure. Due to a combination of factors, the government of Uzbekistan closed the military base in Hanabad in the fall of 2005.

War on International Terrorism

⋀ US military bases

⋀ Russian military bases

Power base of IMU

Power base of Hizb-Ut-Tahrir

Map 48: Border Disputes in the Farghona Valley

Since the 1980s the Farghona Valley has been potentially one of the most explosive areas in Central Asia, and a microcosm also of the social, political and economic trends typical in the developing world. The Farghona area, which occupies less than four percent of the region's territory, is home to about 15 percent of the region's population. It is shared between three republics—Kyrgyzstan, Tajikistan and Uzbekistan—and therefore destabilization in the valley can immediately affect all three republics. This is particularly true for Uzbekistan, whose capital, Tashkent, the largest urban center in the region, is situated roughly 100 miles (160 kilometers) away. All the problems and conflicts that have affected the region since independence are to be found in the valley (Rubin 1999).

In many ways the problems in the valley replicate patterns of development in countless agriculture-based third world countries. Over the past 50 years the population in the area has nearly tripled, reaching between 8 and 9 million. Due to this massive demographic expansion in the 1970s and 1980s, the valley's population is largely youthful, with an estimated 45 to 50 percent 28 years old or younger. This growth has severely aggravated competition for resources and jobs between individuals and communities. Social problems have become particularly acute, as local and national governments did not direct adequate investment into job-creation in the 1980s and the 1990s. According to various estimates, between 15 and 30 percent of the people in the area are unemployed or underemployed and about half the population lives below the poverty line (International Crisis Group 2000). Limited market-oriented reforms and the opening of private initiatives have been introduced only in the Kyrgyzstan and Tajikistan parts of the Farghona Valley, not on the Uzbekistan side.

The area's social and demographic problems have been worsened by an ecological crisis. The Farghona Valley is one of the most productive agricultural areas in the region, but it has a very fragile ecosystem. As in many developing countries, local peasants tend to use outdated practices and technologies in order to squeeze out of their small plots of land as much produce as possible, often ignoring long-term consequences. Thus, the valley has lost nearly all of its alpine and subalpine forest, and large areas of bush along the rivers and creeks have also been destroyed. This in turn has led to an increase in the frequency of landslides and floods during the wet season, water shortages in the dry season and severe salinization and desertification.

Competition between communities has been aggravated even further by the multiethnic composition of the area and by rising nationalism. It is not uncommon for a small conflict or disagreement between communities to explode into a full-scale confrontation between representatives of different ethnic groups. This type of escalation can immediately involve much larger groups, as neighboring villagers rush to help their kin. Such was the case in community conflicts that led to mass riots claiming many lives in 1988, 1989 and 1990, and in minor water and land disputes in the 1990s.

Economic management and proper governance of the area have been undermined by the erection of borders, a rise in border disputes and an absence of cross-border cooperation. During the Soviet era, all communication, transportation, energy and water infrastructure was built by the central government. After 1991, however, the national governments asserted their sovereign rights over land, property and infrastructure and began managing and using these resources according to their own needs, often ignoring the needs of the others. The case of water management illustrates the problem. The governments of Kyrgyzstan and Tajikistan claim that their water resources constitute proprietary commercial assets and therefore that a downstream country—in this case, Uzbekistan—should pay for the water or let them use the water according to their needs. Kyrgyzstan's and Tajikistan's governments wish to develop hydroelectric power stations and sell the resulting power to China and Afghanistan for hard currency. To accomplish this, Kyrgyzstan and Tajikistan have insisted on their right to manage the water resources by themselves, accumulating as much water as possible during the spring and summer seasons when the demand for electricity is low, and discharging as much as possible in the winter when demand is high. The government of Uzbekistan, on the other hand, has taken the view that water is not a commercial asset but a public good, and hence it has the right to participate in managing the water resources and to use them without having to pay for them. The issue is very important for Uzbekistan, as its cotton farmers need water in the spring and summer, while excessive water during the winters would flood their fields.

In the meantime, as local and national governments have been locked in unending disputes and inefficient practices, various radical Islamist groups have stepped in. These groups claim that the only solution lies in their vision of radical change, which includes building Taliban-style governments and legal systems. These groups are believed to have established close ties with the Taliban and to have undergone training in their camps. Upon returning from Afghanistan, they went so far as to attempt the seizure of villages and towns in remote areas of Kyrgyzstan, Tajikistan and Uzbekistan in order to establish their presence and power bases there. All together this development added a whole new layer of tension to the existing situation, further destabilizing the area.

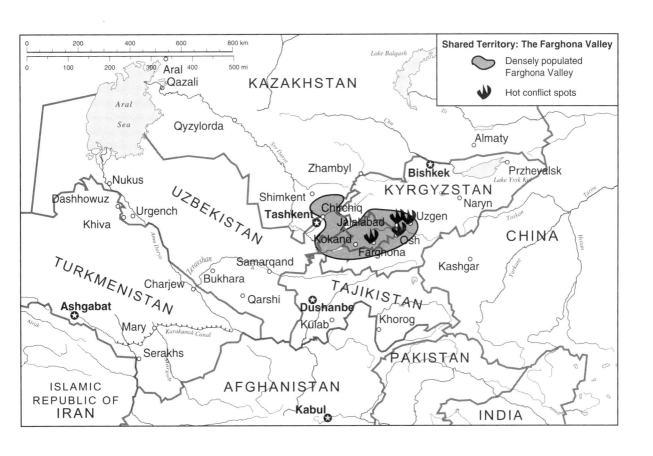

Map 49: Major Oil and Gas Pipeline Proposals

Throughout the 1990s, multibillion-dollar oil and gas deals and pipeline contracts completed in Central Asia made headlines in major newspapers. Some commentators hastened to compare the Central Asian energy reserves favorably with those in the Middle East. Yet other experts claim that the region's oil reserves are in fact modest and no match for those in the Middle East. Whoever is right, the region's estimated potential, ranging from a conservative 80 billion barrels of oil to an optimistic 200 billion barrels, is valued at 5 to 7 trillion U.S. dollars at 2003 prices.

Although early small-scale extraction of oil reserves in Central Asia began long before the mid-twentieth century, it took nearly a hundred years for large-scale exploitation to become a reality. Similarly, the region's large gas reserves were discovered after World War Two, but extraction didn't begin until the 1970s. Several factors contributed to these delays: difficult geographic terrain, extremes of continental climate, high seismic activity and remoteness from major consumers in Eastern and Western Europe.

Throughout the Soviet era no foreign companies were allowed to operate in the region. The Kremlin invested a huge amount of money in large-scale commercial exploration of the reserves during and after World War II. The most extensive oil reserves were found on the northern and eastern shores of the Caspian Sea and in central and western Kazakhstan. The largest gas reserves were found in Kazakhstan, Turkmenistan and Uzbekistan. During the Soviet-era the oil was delivered via the pipelines of Shevchenko-Guriev (both Kazakhstan)-Orsk-Ufa (both Russia), Shevchenko-Guriev-Kuibushev, and Shimkent-Pavlodar-Omsk. The gas was delivered via the pipelines of Mary (Turkmenistan)-Khiva (Uzbekistan)-Saratov, Mary-Khiva-Chelyabinsk, and Mary-Khiva-Gazli-Almaty (CIA 1985).

The first negotiations with Western oil and gas companies on possible technology transfers and prospective joint-venture development of some oil fields began in the 1980s. As the First Gulf War was being fought, many international experts and some policy makers began talking about a need to diversify oil supply sources in case of a major crisis in the Middle East. This stimulated interest in, discussion on and speculation about the place of Central Asia and its energy reserves in the international energy market, and potential transportation routes for large-scale exports of those reserves. Dozens of oil and gas pipeline projects were discussed and feasibility studies were conducted in the 1990s. Within this framework, transnational corporations (TNC) developed feasibility studies on several programs: east-west, east-southwest, east-south and east-southeast. These programs projected the development

of oil and gas delivery to Western Europe via Russia, the Caucasus and Turkey; to India and Pakistan via Afghanistan and probably via Iran; and to China and potentially Korea and Japan via China or Russian Siberia. As of 2007 a number of these projects had materialized.

The Caspian Pipeline Consortium (CPC) is intended to bring oil from Kazakhstan's largest oil field at Tenghiz to Novorossiisk, a Russian seaport on the Black Sea. It was established by Chevron, Agip, Mobil and companies representing Kazakhstan, Oman and Russia (the ownership structure has changed over time) in order to construct a 1,500-kilometer-long export-oil pipeline. The first stage was completed in 2001 and it is expected that the second stage, which will triple the pipeline's capacity, will be completed in 2010.

The Baku-Tbilisi-Ceyhan (BTC) pipeline was proposed to bring oil to Turkey's Mediterranean port of Ceyhan and then to the European market, bypassing Russia. It became operational in 2005. The international partners that worked on the BTC also built the South Caucasus Pipeline (SCP), which brought natural gas from the Caspian Sea along the same route via Baku and Tbilisi to the Turkish city of Erzurum and then to the European market. It became operational in 2006.

The Kazakhstan-China Oil Pipeline (KCOP) is intended to bring oil from oil-rich Kazakhstan to the Chinese market. The line's total length will be about 3,000 kilometers, at an estimated cost of 3.5 to 4.9 billion U.S. dollars. This pipeline has been divided into several sections, the last of which will be completed in 2011. The first section, Aktube-Atyrau, was completed in 2003 and the section from Atasu (central Kazakhstan) to Alashankou (western China) was completed in 2005. By 2011 this pipeline is expected to be connected to the Chinese pipeline system running from Xingjian to eastern and south-eastern provinces of the PRC.

The Turkmenistan-Iran-Turkey Gas Pipeline (TITGP) is intended to bring Turkmenistan's gas to western markets through Iran and Turkey. Turkmenistan has already completed a pipeline for exporting small amounts of gas to Iran, but the TITGP project has been delayed by U.S. economic sanctions against Iran and is still in the planning stage. There was an additional project that proposed to deliver Turkmenistan's gas via the trans-Iranian gas pipeline to the Persian Gulf.

The Turkmenistan-Afghanistan-Pakistan-India Gas Pipeline (TAPIGP) is intended to bring gas from Turkmenistan to Pakistan and India. However, this project was undermined by the political instability and war in Afghanistan and therefore had not gone beyond feasibility stage as of 2007.

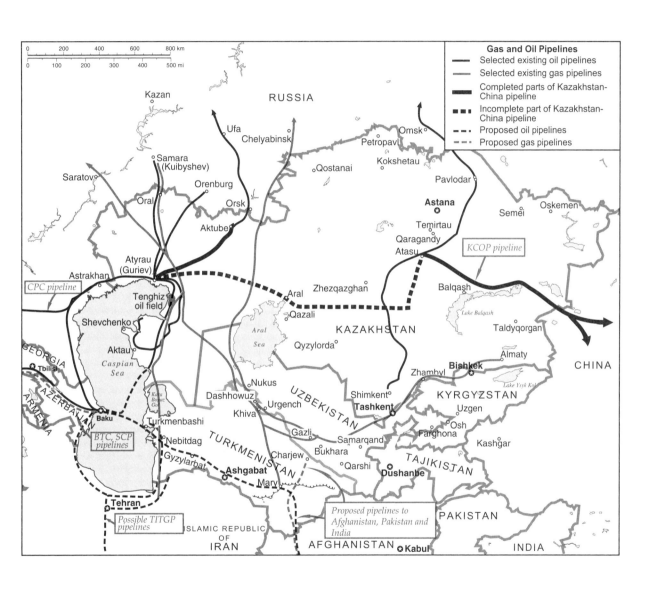

Gas and Oil Pipelines
— Selected existing oil pipelines
— Selected existing gas pipelines
━━ Completed parts of Kazakhstan-China pipeline
▪▪▪ Incomplete part of Kazakhstan-China pipeline
- - Proposed oil pipelines
- - Proposed gas pipelines

RUSSIA

Kazan
Ufa
Chelyabinsk
Omsk
Petropavl
Qostanai
Kokshetau
Pavlodar
Samara (Kuibyshev)
Saratov
Orenburg
Astana
Semĕi
Oskemen
Oral
Orsk
Temirtau
Aktube
Qaragandy
Atasu
KCOP pipeline
Atyrau (Guriev)
Astrakhan
Aral
Zhezqazghan
Balqash
CPC pipeline
Tenghiz oil field
Lake Balqash
Qazali
Shevchenko
Taldyqorgan
Aral Sea
KAZAKHSTAN
Aktau
Caspian Sea
Qyzylorda
Almaty
GEORGIA
Tbilisi
Kara-Bogaz Gol
Zhambyl
Bishkek
CHINA
ARMENIA
Nukus
Shimkent
Lake Ysyk Köl
AZERBAIJAN
Dashhowuz
Urgench
UZBEKISTAN
Tashkent
KYRGYZSTAN
Baku
Khiva
Uzgen
BTC, SCP pipelines
Turkmenbashi
Gazli
Osh
Farghona
Nebitdag
Samarqand
Bukhara
Kashgar
TURKMENISTAN
Charjew
Qarshi
TAJIKISTAN
Gyzylarbat
Ashgabat
Dushanbe
Mary
Tehran
Possible TITGP pipelines
Proposed pipelines to Afghanistan, Pakistan and India
PAKISTAN
ISLAMIC REPUBLIC OF IRAN
AFGHANISTAN
⊕ Kabul
INDIA

0   200   400   600   800 km
0   100   200   300   400   500 mi

Map 50: Transportation Routes

Independence opened up new opportunities for the Central Asian states to join in globalization trends. The Central Asian leaders believed that international trade would help lift them out of the Soviet-era's economic and political isolation.

From the early 1990s the Central Asian governments began talking about a resurrection of the trade through the Great Silk Road (see maps 13 and 21). In the new geopolitical environment, Central Asia could provide several significant advantages if new transportation networks were built. Central Asian infrastructure could provide the shortest overland connection between the growing Chinese and European markets, and it could also connect India and Pakistan with Central Asia, Russia and Eastern Europe. The Central Asian states would boost their lost economic growth as well through access to international transportation networks, reductions in their export costs and the benefits arising from trade.

The development of international trade and transportation infrastructure in the new millennium would require not only the building of new roads but also a reconceptualization of the whole model of regional and subregional trade. This included diversification of transportation networks, reducing dependency on Russia.

To address their existing problems systematically, the Central Asian republics initiated or joined several international programs, consortiums and organizations, including the large transnational concepts of the Eurasian Infrastructure Corridor (EIC), Eurasian Land-Bridge (ELB), Eurasian Railroad Transportation Corridor (ERTC) and Trans-Asiatic Pipeline Network (TAPN). All of these programs were designed to promote the building of comprehensive railroad and pipeline systems. Central Asian leaders, together with leaders of nine states in Eastern Europe and the Caucasus, established a new international organization in 1998 (officially inaugurated in 2001): the Transport Corridor Europe-Caucasus-Central Asia (TRACECA), with a specific mandate to facilitate the development of infrastructure projects within the territories of the member states. Various transportation projects were discussed, studied and developed by the Commonwealth of Independent States (CIS), Economic Cooperation Organization (ECO) and the Shanghai Cooperation Organization (SCO).

The **Transport Corridor Europe-Caucasus-Central Asia** (TRACECA) is designed to optimize the management, usage and development of existing rail and highway systems among the member states. This project is intended to restore and extend the transportation infrastructure that existed during the Soviet era but began falling apart, largely due to the nationalization of various sections of the system by the newly independent states and to the collapse of interstate trade among former Soviet republics. The member states also hope to address the need for development of commerce and trade among members and intraregional trade.

The **Eurasian Railroad Transportation Corridor** (ERTC) is intended to connect the port of Rotterdam in the Netherlands with the Chinese port of Lianyungand on the Yellow Sea, through a Central Asian railroad network that links to the Chinese rail system and the Russian trans-Siberian railroad system. Another phase of the project calls for building a Paris-Shanghai link, using existing railroad infrastructure. This project would mobilize both private and public investment to build the links missing between various sections of the system or reconstruct and update run-down sections. A long-term proposal that would technically make it possible to travel by rail from Western Europe to China, it will probably take decades before commercial exploitation is possible.

The **North-South Transportation Corridor** (NSTC) is intended to connect Central Asia with South Asia via the Karakorum Mountain Road and/or via Afghanistan, thus boosting trade between various remote areas in Kyrgyzstan, Tajikistan, Afghanistan and Pakistan. Although the Osh-Karakorum road was completed, its usage has been undermined by the political instability in Afghanistan. There is also a proposal to build a railroad connecting Osh with Bishkek, thus extending the NSTC to northern Kyrgyzstan and Kazakhstan.

The **North-South Rail-Ship Container Corridor** (NSRSC) is planned to connect northern Europe and industrial centers in northwestern Russia with seaports in the Persian Gulf and potentially with South Asia via the Central Asian republics or the Caspian Sea. This project envisions a combination of river and sea transportation, with overland rail connections on some sections. One variation of the project includes a Russia-Iran-India transportation corridor.

The **Central Asia–Persian Gulf Railway Project (CAPGRP)** is proposed to connect the Central Asian and Iranian railway systems from Mary to Bandar-Abbas seaport in the Persian Gulf. This project was supported by the ECO, and in the late 1990s the connection between the two systems was inaugurated. However, the commercial usage of the project was delayed by a combination of economic recession in Central Asia, Turkmenistan's isolation from the economic integration processes in Central Asia and U.S.-imposed sanctions against Iran.

The **Central Asia-East Asia Highway** (CAEAHW) would link several countries on the Tashkent-Andijon (Uzbekistan)-Osh (Kyrgyzstan)-Kashgar (China) route, boosting intraregional trade. A large section of the road (Tashkent-Andijon-Osh) already exists, and it has been reported that feasibility studies were completed for building the most technologically challenging stretch, between Osh and Kashgar through the Tian Shan Mountains. This project is supported and backed by the SCO.

Selected Bibliography

This bibliography of selected publications on Central Asia will help scholars, students and the general public in their further studies of the region, its people and political and economic development. Most of the works cover Central Asian history in general while others look at its important features or particular periods. Most of them include various historical maps. Currently, several books are available that comprehensively cover the history of Central Asia from the early days to the present, including the most authoritative five-volume work, published under the auspices of UNESCO: *The History of Civilizations of Central Asia* (published between 1996 and 2006). Those who would like to find additional reading might consider turning to the most comprehensive bibliographical work, Yuri Bregel's three-volume *Bibliography of Islamic Central Asia* published in 1995. It contains bibliographical references to thousands of books in English, Russian, French, German, Central Asian and other languages. Considering space limitations, and the scope of the *Palgrave Concise Historical Atlas of Central Asia*, the author chose the most prominent modern works, which can lead readers to other publications, giving priority to the most recent atlases and publications that include useful maps. Moreover, in the age of information technology many websites provide useful Internet links, bibliographies, and access to historical documents, memoirs and travel reports, as well as links to historical and political maps and statistical data for further studies of Central Asia. In this section readers will also find a concise list of Internet resources. The author is fully aware that there are hundreds and hundreds of volumes published on the topic in the Central Asian and Russian languages; however, the author included only a few of them, hoping that readers will find appropriate publications in specialized libraries, archives and collections.

Abazov, Rafis. *Historical Dictionary of Kyrgyzstan*. Lanham, Md.: Scarecrow Press, 2004.

———, *Historical Dictionary of Turkmenistan*. Lanham, Md.: Scarecrow Press, 2005.

Adle, Chahryar, Mahdavan K. Palat, and Anara Tabyshalieva. *History of Civilizations of Central Asia*. Paris: UNESCO, 2005.

Adle, Chahryar, Irfan Habib, and Karl M. Baipakov. *History of Civilizations of Central Asia. Development in Contrast: from the Sixteenth to the Mid-Nineteenth Century*. Paris: UNESCO, 2004.

Adshead, Samuel. *Central Asia in World History*. London: Macmillan, 1993.

Akiner, Shirin. *Islamic People of the Soviet Union*. London: Kegan Paul International, 1983.

Akiner, Shirin, ed. *The Caspian: Politics, Energy and Security*. London and New York: Routledge Curzon, 2004.

Allworth, Edward, ed. *Central Asia: 130 Years of Russian Dominance. A Historical Overview*. Durham, N.C.: Duke University Press, 1994.

"Almaty Declaration." In: "Report of the International Ministerial Conference of Landlocked and Transit Developing Countries and Donor Countries and International Financial and Development Institutions On Transit Cooperation, Almaty, Kazakhstan, 28 and 29 August 2003." New York: UN, 2003, pp. 24–26 (UN document A/CONF.202/3).

Alram, Michael, and Deborah E. Klimburg-Salter, eds. *Coins, Art, and Chronology: Essays on pre-Islamic History of the Indo-Iranian Borderlands*. Vienna: Österreichischen Akademie der Wissenschaften, 1999.

Bartold, Vasilii V. *Cultural History of the Muslims*. (Translated from the Russian by Shahid Suhrawardy.) New Delhi: Mittal Publications, 1995.

———, *Turkestan Down to the Mongol Invasion*. London: Luzac, 1928.

Benningsen, Alexandre, and Chantal Lemercier-Quelquejay. *Islam in the Soviet Union*. New York: Praeger, 1967.

Biran, Michal. *Qaidu and the Rise of the Independent Mongol State in Central Asia*. London: Routledge, 1997.

———. *The Empire of the Qara Khitai in Eurasian History. Between China and the Islamic World*. Cambridge: Cambridge University Press, 2005.

Bosworth, Clifford Edmund, and M. S. Asimov. *History of Civilizations of Central Asia. The Age of Achievement: A.D. 750 to the End of the Fifteenth Century*. Paris: UNESCO, 2004.

Boyle, J. A., ed. *Cambridge History of Iran*. Cambridge: Cambridge University Press, 1968.

Bregel, Yuri. *An Historical Atlas of Central Asia* (Handbook of Oriental Studies/Handbuch Der Orientalistik – Part 8: Uralic & Central Asian Studies, 9). Brill Academic Publishers, 2003.

Bregel, Yuri, ed. *Historical Maps of Central Asia: 9th–19th Centuries*. Bloomington, Ind.: Research Institute for Inner Asian Studies, 2000.

Breton, Roland J.-L. *Atlas of the Languages and Ethnic Communities of South Asia*. Thousand Oaks, Ca.: Sage Publications, 1997.

Brice, William C., and Hugh Kennedy. *An Historical Atlas of Islam* (*Encyclopaedia of Islam New Edition*). Leiden: Brill, 1981.

Central Intelligence Agency. *USSR Energy Atlas*. Washington, D.C.: Central Intelligence Agency, 1985.

Channon, John, and Robert Hudson. *The Penguin Historical Atlas of Russia*. London; New York: Viking, 1995.

Clubb, O. E. *China and Russia: The "Great Game."* New York: Columbia University Press, 1971.

Colledge, Malcolm. *The Parthians*. New York: Praeger, 1967.

Crandall, Maureen. *Energy, Economics and Politics in the Caspian Region: Dream and Reality*. Westport, Conn.; London: Praeger Security International, 2006.

Crews, Robert. *For Prophet and Tsar: Islam and Empire in Russia and Central Asia*. Cambridge, Mass.: Harvard University Press, 2006.

Cummings, Sally N., ed. *Oil, Transition and Security in Central Asia*. New York: Routledge, 2003.

Curtis, Glen, ed. *Kazakhstan, Kyrgyzstan, Tajikistan, Turkmenistan, and Uzbekistan: Country Studies (Area Handbook Series)*. Washington, D.C.: Federal Research Division, Library of Congress, 1997.

Curzon, George Nathaniel. *The Pamirs and the Source of the Oxus*. London: Royal Geographic Society, 1896.

———. *Russia in Central Asia in 1889 and the Anglo-Russian Question*. London: Cass, repr. 1967.

Danmore, the Earl. *The Pamirs. Being A Narrative of a Year's Expedition on Horseback and on Foot Through Kashmir, Western Tibet, Chinese Tartary, and Russian Central Asia*. 2 vols. London: John Murray, 1893.

Demko, George J. *The Russian Colonization of Kazakhstan, 1896–1916*. Bloomington: Indiana University Press, 1969.

Feshbach, Murray, and Alfred Friendly. *Ecocide in the USSR: Health and Nature under Siege*. New York: Basic Books, 1992.

Findley, Carter Vaughn. *The Turks in World History*. New York: Oxford University Press, 2005.

Firdowsi, Abolqasem. *Shahnameh: The Persian Book of Kings*. Trans. Dick Davis. New York: Viking Adult, 2006.

Foltz, Richard C. *Religions of the Silk Road: Overland Trade and Cultural Exchange from Antiquity to the Fifteenth Century*. New York: St. Martin's Press, 1999.

Gafurov, Bobozhan. *Central Asia: Pre-Historic to Modern Time*. (English Translation) Introduction by Devendra Kaushik. Delhi, India: Shirpa Publications, 2005.

Geiss, Paul Georg. *Pre-Tsarist and Tsarist Central Asia: Communal Commitment and Political Order in Change*. London; New York: Routledge Curzon, 2003.

Gibb, H. A. R. *The Travels of Ibn Battuta*. London: 1929; repr. 2000.

———. *The Arab Conquest of Central Asia*. London: 1923; repr. 1970.

Gibbon, Edward. *The History of the Decline and Fall of the Roman Empire*. New York: Blue Unicorn Editions, 2001.

Gilbert, Martin. *The Routledge Atlas of Russian History*. Third Edition. London; New York; Routledge, 2002.

Golden, Peter. *An Introduction to the History of the Turkic Peoples*. Wiesbaden: Otto Harrassassowitz, 1992.

Haidar, Mansura. *Indo-Central Asian Relations: From Early Times to Medieval Period*. New Delhi; Manohar, 2004.

Haidar, Mirza Muhammad. *The Tarikh-i-Rashidi* [A History of the Moghuls of Central Asia]. English trans. E. Denison Ross. (1895). Patna: Academica Asiatica, repr. 1973.

Hauner, Milan. *What is Asia for Us? Russia's Asian Heartland Yesterday and Today*. Boston; London: Unwin Hyman, 1990.

Haywood, John, and Simon Hall. *The Penguin Historical Atlas of Ancient Civilizations (Penguin Historical Atlas)*. New York: Penguin (Non-Classics), 2005.

Hedin, Sven. *Central Asia Atlas, Memoir on Maps*. Stockholm: the Sven Hedin Foundation, Statens etnografiska museum, 1967.

Hemming, John. *The Oxford Atlas of Exploration*. Oxford; New York: Oxford University Press, 1997.

Herodotus. *The Histories*. Trans. A. D. Godley. Cambridge, Ma.: Harvard University Press, 1963–1969.

Hoff, Brent, and Carter Smith. *Mapping Epidemics: A Historical Atlas of Disease*. Franklin Watts, 2000.

Hopkirk, Peter. *The Great Game: the Struggle for Empire in Central Asia*. New York: Kodansha International, 1992.

Iacomelli, Aldo. *Renewable Energies for Central Asia Countries: Economic, Environmental and Social Impacts (NATO Science Series: IV: Earth and Environmental Sciences)*. Springer, 2006.

International Crisis Group. *Central Asia: Crisis Conditions in Three States*. Brussels and Osh: International Crisis Group, 2000.

Johnson, Gordon. *Cultural Atlas of India: India, Pakistan, Nepal, Bhutan, Bangladesh & Sri Lanka*. New York: Facts on File, 1996.

Kaiser, R. J. *The Geography of Nationalism in Russia and the USSR*. Princeton, N.J.: Princeton University Press, 1994.

Kashgari, Mahmud. In: Dankoff, R., and J. Kelly. *Compendium of the Turkic Dialects*, vol. 1. Cambridge, Mass.: Harvard University Press, 1982.

Khan, Aisha. *A Historical Atlas of Kyrgyzstan* (Historical Atlases of South Asia, Central Asia and the Middle East). New York: Rosen Publishing Group, 2004.

———. *A Historical Atlas of Uzbekistan* (Historical Atlases of South Asia, Central Asia and the Middle East). New York: Rosen Publishing Group, 2003.

———. *A Historical Atlas of India* (Historical Atlases of South Asia, Central Asia and the Middle East). New York: Rosen Publishing Group, 2003.

Khazanov, Anatoly. *Nomads and the Outside World*. Trans. Julia Crookenden. Madison: University of Wisconsin Press, 1994.

Knobloch, Edgar. *Beyond the Oxus. Archaeology, Art and Architecture of Central Asia*. London: Ernest, 1972.

Komroff, Manuel. *Contemporaries of Marco Polo*. London: 1928; repr. 1989.

Kwanten, Luc. *Imperial Nomads. A History of Central Asia, 500–1500*. Philadelphia: University of Pennsylvania Press, 1979.

Lattimore, Owen, and Eleanor Lattimore. *Silk, Spices and Empire: Asia Seen through the Eyes of Its Discoverers*. New York: Dell, 1968.

Lewis, Bernard. *Islam in History: Ideas, People, and Events in the Middle East.* Second Edition. Chicago: Open Court, 2001.

Lewis, Robert A., Robert R. Churchill, and Amanda Tate. *Geographic Perspectives on Soviet Central Asia.* New York: Routledge, 1992.

Manz, Beatrice F., ed. *Central Asia in Historical Perspective.* Boulder, Colo.: Westview Press, 1993.

Manz, Beatrice F. *Rise and Rule of Tamerlane.* Cambridge: Cambridge University Press, repr. 2002.

McGovern, W. M. *The Early History of Central Asia. A Study of the Scythians and the Huns and the Part They Played in World History.* Chapel Hill: University of North Carolina Press, 1939.

Milner-Gulland, Robin, and Nikolai Dejevsky. *Cultural Atlas of Russia and the Former Soviet Union.* New York: Checkmark Books, 1998.

Neilson, Keith. *Britain and the Last Tsar: British Policy and Russia, 1894–1917.* New York: Oxford University Press, 1995.

Nicolle, David. *Historical Atlas of the Islamic World.* New York: Checkmark Books, 2003.

Olcott, Brill Martha. *The Kazakhs.* 2nd ed. Stanford, Ca.: Stanford University Press, 1995.

Onians, John. *Atlas of World Art.* London: Laurence King, 2004.

Pahlen, K. K. *Mission to Turkestan.* London: Oxford University Press, 1964.

Parks, George B., ed. *The Book of Ser Marco Polo, the Venetian.* New York: Macmillan, 1927.

Perdue, Peter. *China Marches West: The Qing Conquest of Central Eurasia.* Cambridge, Mass.: Belknap Press of Harvard University Press, 2005.

Pierce, Richard. *Russian Central Asia, 1867–1917: A Study of Colonial Rule.* Berkeley: University of California Press, 1960.

Rashid al-Din Tabib. *The Successors of Genghis Khan.* Trans. John Andrew Boyle. New York: Columbia University Press, 1971.

Rawlington, (Sir) Henry. *England and Russia in the East.* London, 1875; repr. New York: Praeger, 1970.

Rayfield, Donald. *The Dream of Lhasa: The Life of Nikolay Przhevalsky (1839–88): Explorer of Central Asia.* London: Elek, 1976.

Rockhill, W. *The Journey of William Rubruck to the Eastern Parts of the World, 1253–1255.* London: 1900; repr. 1998.

Romano, Amy. *A Historical Atlas of Afghanistan (Historical Atlases of South Asia, Central Asia, and the Middle East).* New York: Rosen Publishing Group, 2003.

Rossabi, Morris. *China and Inner Asia: From 1368 to the Present Day (Chinese History and Society).* New York: Pica Press, 1975.

Ruthven, Malise, and Azim Nanji. *Historical Atlas of Islam.* Cambridge, Mass.: Harvard University Press, 2004.

Rubin, Barnett, and Nancy Lubin. *Calming the Ferghana Valley: Development and Dialogue in the Heart of Central Asia.* New York: Century Foundation Press, 1999.

Rywkin, Michael. *Moscow's Muslim Challenge.* London: C. Hurst, 1982.

Santon, Kate, and Liz McKay. *Atlas of World History*. Bath: Parragon Book, 2005.

Schuyler, Eugene. *Turkistan*. 2 vols. New York: Charles Scribner's, 1876.

Semenov, Petr Petrovich. *Travels in the Tian'-Shan' 1856–1857*. Ed. Colin Thomas; trans. Liudmila Gilmour, Colin Thomas, and Marcus Wheeler. London: Hakluyt Society, 1998.

Sima, Qian. *Records of the Grand Historian. Han Dynasty*. Trans. Burton Watson. New York: Renditions-Columbia University Press, 1993.

Sinor, Denis. *The Cambridge History of Early Inner Asia*. Cambridge, UK: Cambridge University Press, 1990.

———. *Inner Asia and Its Contacts with Medieval Europe*. London: Variorum Reprints, 1977.

Skrine, F. H., and E. Ross. *The Heart of Asia. A History of Russian Turkestan and the Central Asian Khanates from Earliest Times*. London: Methuen, 1893.

Soucek, Svat. *A History of Inner Asia*. Cambridge, UK: Cambridge University Press, 2000.

Swift, Jonathan. *Palgrave Concise Historical Atlas of the Cold War*. New York: Palgrave Macmillan, 2004.

Taylor, Bayard. *Central Asia. Travels in Cashmere, Little Tibet and Central Asia*. Comp. and arranged by Bayard Taylor. New York, Scribner, Armstrong, and Co., 1874; repr. Scholarly Publishing Office, University of Michigan Library, 2005.

Tracy, James D. *The Rise of Merchant Empires: Long-Distance Trade in the Early Modern World, 1350–1750*. Cambridge, UK; New York: Cambridge University Press, 1990.

Tucker, Jonathan, and Antonia Tozer. *The Silk Road: Art and History*. London: Philip Wilson, 2003.

United Nations Economic Commission for Europe. *Environmental Performance Reviews: Kyrgyzstan*. New York: United Nations, 2000.

United Nations Economic and Social Commission for Asia and the Pacific. *Atlas of Mineral Resources of the ESCAP Region: Geology and Mineral Resources of Kyrgyzstan*. New York: United Nations Publications, 2000.

Vamberi, Arminius. *Sketches of Central Asia: Additional Chapters on My Travels, Adventures, and on the Ethnology of Central Asia*. London: W. A. Allen, 1868.

———. *Travels to Central Asia; Being the Account of a Journey from Teheran across the Turkoman Desert on the Eastern Shore of the Caspian to Khiva, Bokhara, and Samarkand, Performed in the Year 1863*. London: J. Murray, 1864.

———. *History of Bukhara*. New York: Arno, 1973.

Vernadsky, George. *The Mongols and Russia*. New Haven; London: Yale University Press, 1953.

Wessels, C. *Early Jesuit Travelers in Central Asia, 1603–1721*. The Hague: M. Nijhoff, 1924.

Whitfield, Susan, and Ursula Sims-Williams, eds. *The Silk Road: Trade, Travel, War and Faith*. London: British Library, 2004.

Internet Resources

Central Asia and Caucasus Resources (Columbia University): *http://www.sipa.columbia.edu/ece/CACR/index.html*

Central Asia-Caucasus Institute (John Hopkins University): *http://www.cacianalyst.org/index.php*

CIA World Factbook: *https://www.cia.gov/cia/publications/factbook/index.html*

International Crisis Group: *http://www.crisisweb.org/*

Library of Congress Country Studies: *http://lcweb2.loc.gov/frd/cs/list.html*

Maps of the World: *http://www.mapsofworld.com/central-asia-political-map.html*

National Geographic's World Music Page: *http://worldmusic.nationalgeographic.com/worldmusic/view/page.basic/home*

Perry-Castañeda Library Map Collection (University of Texas): *http://www.lib.utexas.edu/maps/asia.html*

Program on Humanitarian Policy and Conflict Research (Harvard School of Public Health): *http://www.preventconflict.org/portal/centralasia/maps.php*

The Times of Central Asia: *http://www.times.kg*

Turkmenistan.ru (Internet Newspaper): *http://www.turkmenistan.ru/*

The Silk Road and Central Asia (University of Washington): *http://depts.washington.edu/reecas/outreach/silklink.htm*

The Silk Road Project: *http://silkroadproject.org/*

United Nations Cartography Department: *http://www.un.org/Depts/Cartographic/english/htmain.htm*

United Nations Environmental Program: *http://maps.grida.no/go/search Region/regionid/geocasia/?country=centralasia*

U.S. Department of State: *http://www.state.gov/p/eur/rt/cacen/*

In Russian and Other Languages

Academy of Science of the Kyrgyz SSR. *Atlas Kirgizskoi Sovetskoi Sotsialisticheskoi Respubliki* [Atlas of the Kyrgyz Soviet Socialist Republic]. Moscow: Glavnoe upravlenie geodezii i kartografii pri Sovete ministrov SSSR, 1987.

Atlas Mira [The Atlas of the World].Moscow: Glavnoe upravlenie geodezii i kartografii, 1985.

Atlas SSSR [The Atlas of the USSR]. Moscow: Glavnoe upravlenie geodezii i kartografii, 1985.

Baratov, et al. *Atlas Tadzhikskoi Sovetskoi Sotsialisticheskoi Respubliki* [The Atlas of the Tajik Soviet Socialist Republic]. Dushanbe and Moscow: [s.n.], 1968.

Bazilevich, K.V., I.A. Golubtsova, and M.A. Zinoveva. eds. *Atlas istorii SSSR*. [The Atlas of the History of the USSR]. 3 vols. Moscow: Glavnoe upravlenie geodezii i kartografii, 1950–1954.

Istoria Kazakhskoi SSR s drevneishikh vremen do nashikh dnei [The History of the Kazakh SSR from Ancient Time to Present Days]. 5 vols. Almaty: Nauka, 1976–1979.

Istoria Uzbekskoi SSR [The History of the Uzbek SSR]. 4 vols. Tashkent: Fan, 1965–1968.

Kafesoglu, Ibrahim. Turk Bozkir Kulturu (Turkish Steppe Culture). Ankara: Turk Kulturunu Arastirma Enstitusu, 1987.

Muminov, Ibragim M., ed. *Istoriia Samarkanda* [The History of Samarqand]. 2 vols. Tashkent: Fan, 1969–1970.

Rhins, J.-L. Dutreuil de. *L'Asie centrale (Thibet et régions limitrophes)*. Paris: E. Leroux, 1889.

Saray, Mehmet. *Yeni Turk Cumhuriyetleri Tarihi* [The History of the New Central Asian Republics]. Ankara: Turk Tarih Kurumu Basimevi, 1996.

Tolstov, S. P. *Drevnii Khorezm* [Ancient Khorezm]. Moscow: [s.n.] 1949.

Turkish Cultural Service Foundation. *Türk dünyası kültür atlası.* [A Cultural Atlas of the Turkish World]. Istanbul: Turkish Cultural Service Foundation, 1997.

Index

About the Author

Rafis Abazov is an Adjunct Assistant Professor at the Harriman Institute/School of International and Public Affairs at Columbia University, New York. Rafis Abazov's area of expertise is in the field of modern Central Asian and Russian/Soviet politics and history. His research and teaching interests include public policy and governance, the history of cultural development and population movement in the Russian Empire and Soviet Union with a focus on Central Asia, and comparative history of Central Asia and the Middle East. He was awarded the NATO research fellowship for research on foreign policy formation in Central Asia; the Institute of Advanced Studies of the United Nations University research fellowship and a British Academy visiting fellowship.

Rafis Abazov has written five books and a number of other publications on economic and political development in Eurasia. His most recent books include *Historical Dictionary of Kyrgyzstan* (Scarecrow Press, 2004), *Historical Dictionary of Turkmenistan* (Scarecrow Press, 2005), *The Culture and Customs of the Central Asian Republics* (Greenwood Press, 2007) and *The Culture and Customs of Turkey* (Greenwood Press, 2008). His research articles were published in various academic journals including *Eurasian Studies, The Central Asian Survey, Nationalities Papers, Post-Communist Economies* and some others. He has also contributed articles to the *Encyclopaedia of Modern Asia* (2003), the *Encyclopaedia of Nationalism* (2001), the *Encyclopaedia of National Economies* (2002) and some others.